T0350513

Branded Entertainment

Dealmaking Strategies & Techniques for Industry Professionals

Damaris Valero

J.ROSS

PUBLISHING

ISBN-13: 978-1-60427-094-5

Printed and bound in the U.S.A. Printed on acid-free paper

10 9 8 7 6 5 4 3 2 1

Library of Congress Cataloging-in-Publication Data
Valero, Damaris, 1966-
  Branded entertainment : dealmaking strategies and techniques for industry
professionals / by Damaris Valero.
     pages cm
  Includes index.
  ISBN 978-1-60427-094-5 (hardcover : alk. paper) 1. Branding (Marketing)
2. Brand name products. 3. Mass media and publicity. 4.
Television—Production and direction. 5. Motion pictures—Production and
direction. I. Title.
  HF5415.1255.V35 2014
  658.8′27—dc23
                              2014029054

This publication contains information obtained from authentic and highly
regarded sources. Reprinted material is used with permission, and sources are
indicated. Reasonable effort has been made to publish reliable data and information, but the author and the publisher cannot assume responsibility for the
validity of all materials or for the consequences of their use.

Direct all inquiries to J. Ross Publishing, Inc., 300 S. Pine Island Road,
Suite #305, Plantation, FL 33324.

Phone: (954) 727-9333
Fax: (561) 892-0700
web: www.jrosspub.com

To my father, Marcos Valero (1941–2009),
for teaching me no limits in my career and for
showing me how to use my instincts in business

Contents

Foreword

Relentless. Fearless. Transformational.

In the world of Branded Entertainment these aren't just words, they're the essence, the mantra, that leaders in this space must follow to succeed. This mantra does not end with just a single advocate championing the goals. It must be embraced by all key participants—the clients, agencies, production companies, and media partners: *relentless* with innovation in designing Branded Entertainment experiences that go beyond product integration; *fearless* with new media and understanding the multi-platforms where Branded Entertainment engages beyond a sixty-second spot; and *transformational* with providing experiences that change human behavior and increase brand loyalty.

As Damaris Valero and I got to know each other, I quickly learned she not only possesses these qualities, but she also lives by them. We have built a professional relationship based on mutual respect and admiration as pioneers in this space of Branded Entertainment that ensures we could not only create a Branded Entertainment opportunity that was mutually beneficial, but that we could also have the potential for long-term success and consumer engagement.

This book lays the foundation for what is needed to succeed in Branded Entertainment. It discusses key elements such as what Branded Entertainment is, what it isn't, how Branded Entertainment deals can be structured, and what makes them successful. The book also encapsulates key learnings that have taken years and numerous projects to effectively produce. In essence, the information in this book can translate into a substantial head start for you and your organization. It applies what Damaris has learned through years of experimentation and her relentless pursuit of content, brand, and consumer success.

Inspiration is the foundation of creativity. At the advertising agency where I work, I am surrounded by colleagues who are relentless, fearless, and transformational in everything they set out to accomplish. Their work attributes are the inspiration that continues to elevate the best-in-class practice of Branded Entertainment to new levels. Just like Damaris, I continue to strive to align the ever-changing media marketplace, content voids, and consumer and client needs in a dynamic manner that leads the marketplace and takes Branded Entertainment to new heights. I am so pleased to have Damaris as a partner in the industry with whom to do it.

Take the mantra of relentless, fearless, and transformational and the learnings and ideas outlined in this book and apply them to your specific business. Become a leader and champion for this space. Be inspired. Create something by being relentless, fearless, and transformational. You can do it!

—**Lia Silkwort**
Senior Vice President
Starcom Mediavest Group
Chicago, Illinois

Acknowledgments

Gratefulness and appreciation. These two words sum up what I genuinely feel for those who have stood by me throughout a life filled up with a colorful career.

I will start with my dear sister and mother. They are my pillars and continue to be so regardless! To my dear brothers, Marcos and Salomon, thank you for believing in me at all times. I have learned from your vision, courage, and willingness to stand up and walk again no matter how difficult obstacles get.

I thank Haydee and Norberto for being the two most amazing people I know. Their unbreakable faith is my rock every single day.

Jimmy, I am grateful to you for not letting me forget why I am here doing what I am doing and for letting me be who I truly am. Thank you for your unconditional love.

I also want to thank those who I feel so fortunate to have done business with—I consider you true champs. You are leaders who believe in stepping out of the norm and being the creators of something new. Thank you, Lia Silkworth, Yana Kershteyn, Diane Librizzi, Sandra Alfaro, Oswald Mendez, and Manny Vidal for believing in doing more and breaking the norm. A special thanks to Juan Alfonso for step-ping up and raising the bar at ESPN.

And thanks to those business colleagues who continu-ously inspire me to be better at what I do: Margie Gilmore, Lorna Salazar, Cibele Salomao, Madeline Fuste, Kelly Hirano, Rita Herring, Alvaro Saralegui, Billy Walker, J. C. Acosta, and my friends in Mexico from *El Diez*. You are relentless and true believers in outstanding work.

Thanks to many others whose names I have not men-tioned here, but who have still impacted me throughout my career. I am grateful to all for being true partners and for giving me such great support throughout this journey. Please keep making your work an inspiration for newcomers in the industry today.

And thanks to Ron Martirano and Carolyn Lea for help-ing me make this a better book for industry professionals and to Steve Buda, my publisher, for taking a chance on an industry ready for this book. I look forward to our success.

Introduction

AND NOW BACK TO OUR SPONSOR?

After a long day of work, you sit down in front of the television, cue up the DVR menu, and jump into your favorite procedural crime drama two days after it originally aired. You fast-forward through the opening credits and the first bank of commercials and then sink into the couch as the case of the week unfolds. Just before the second commercial break the female lead uncovers a gruesome piece of evidence while out in the field, away from the rest of her team back at the station. The music comes to a crash as the camera lingers for an extra second on her bloody discovery before the launch of the paid messages that helped make this hour of entertainment possible. You fast-forward again, and when the program returns, the heroine has taken out her camera phone so she can share her findings with her colleagues, connecting the unit back at the stations with shared information delivered instantly and in high definition.

Which advertised products stayed in your mind—the quick, fast-forwarded ones that you quickly glanced at in between segments or the high-definition pictures that deciphered the end of the final scene?

Branded Entertainment was not a fully defined field of entertainment and brands when I started to dabble in it. Branded Entertainment was a concept, an experimental concept, with little information about how to create a deal out of it. The roles of those who were interested in Branded Entertainment were fuzzy. The center of attention was merely on the creative. Back then, if an idea worked creatively, you assumed that a deal would subsequently be consummated, but the reality was that no one really seemed to know how to put all the pieces together.

Branded Entertainment is one of those up-and-coming movements in which the movers and shakers create an illusion of having knowledge when, in reality, their understanding of the principles, commandments, and functionalities is limited. Not much up-to-date information has been readily available to rip through this veil of illusion and limited knowledge. Even today only a few can decipher what Branded Entertainment means to a brand and what it means to the entertainment industry.

Some leaders in the industry have "come to know" mostly by trial and error: the many procedures that did not work created the ones that did. There are only a few authorities on the subject and they are recognized because they tend to carry "on their foreheads" more of the don'ts than the do's of this business. Fortunately, the good news is that we are finally moving to a time when the do's are becoming more refined, defined, and disclosed to all who are desperately seeking a business model. Because the champions are scattered throughout the multiple disciplines of the industry, and they each carry partial information, this book attempts to unite these forces and create formulas that will better define the guidelines and procedures to follow in Branded Entertainment negotiations as the industry and technology continue to evolve.

The primary goal of this book is to paint the clearest picture yet of how the business model functions and what it needs to "come together." Each party plays a pivotal role. This book will explore how each party can best function in a branded ecosystem. The key to the formula is variation. Each deal will continue to have its own uniqueness, but now with a thought process behind it.

Chapter 1 will flesh out the definition of Branded Entertainment, showing what it is and what it is not. Particular attention will be paid to the history of the media that made Branded Entertainment not only a viable option today, but also a necessary one to survive in the days ahead.

Chapter 2 will start to look at how Branded Entertainment is being applied (or misapplied) today and begin to lay the groundwork for an understanding of how a Branded Entertainment deal comes together. Many of the must-have elements that are the subject of later chapters will be introduced.

Chapter 3 will introduce the players who make everything happen in a Branded Entertainment deal. Specific attention will be paid to how these players should be approached and how they might interact with each other.

Chapter 4 will move the discussion forward by focusing on the essential pieces needed to get a Branded Entertainment deal off the ground, from the idea to the necessary paperwork. Then Chapter 5 will take a closer look at the deal itself and how it is moved forward.

Chapter 6 will address the money behind the deal. Chapter 7 puts the whole process together, including a discussion of metrics and how to evaluate the success of our labors.

Chapter 8 contains a case study in which an independent content developer leads the deal. In the case scenario, the producers need to fill a void of scripted content that a network has encountered for several years.

Chapter 9 provides a sample term sheet document. This document outlines some basic guidelines for beginning the process of a potential branded deal between the initiating parties.

About the Author

 Damaris Valero has been the Founder and Executive Producer at Animus Entertainment Group since 2003. Animus Group is a multimedia content provider company with offices in New York, Miami, and Bogota focusing on television production, Branded Entertainment, and program development. Over 80% of Animus productions earn prime-time slots on networks such as Disney Interactive, ESPN, FOX, E!, Telemundo, Televisa, and Univision. Her career in the television industry spans more than 25 years. Her expertise and "know how" have become a symbol of leadership in the industry. Damaris has developed numerous multi-layered deals and has co-produced innovative programming ideas for networks and national advertisers through unique Branded Entertainment formulas.

Damaris has had a successful career launching prime-time television series and cable and digital channels, building joint ventures between companies, and developing content with global groups such as the BBC, the NFL, and Endemol. Her television career began at NBC's Universal Network

Telemundo when she pioneered the international distribution of content to Latin America. Later, she was called upon to start up MTV Networks in Latin America, helping make MTV the #1 advertising-funded network with the largest distribution in Latin America after ESPN.

Damaris started Animus Group as an independent television production operation over a decade ago (2003). She has been a leader in the Branded Entertainment arena by concluding over 20 deals with companies such as ESPN, FOX, NBC, and Univision. For over a decade, she has executive-produced award-winning prime-time series, formats, and movies. Some of her television/film/digital content credits include *Catfish* for MTV in Latin America, Season 1, an observational reality series; *Citizen Kid* for Disney Interactive, Season 1, a docu-reality series; *Kids' Choice Awards* for Nickelodeon in Colombia, an awards show; *That's Fresh* for Disney Jr., Seasons 3 and 4, a lifestyle series for children and parents; *El Diez* for ESPN Deportes, a scripted soccer drama series; *Aaron Loves NY* for FOX Lifestyle, a lifestyle series; *Letra y Musica* for NBC/Telemundo, a docu-reality show about singer/songwriters; *El Juego Supremo* for Univision, a prime-time soccer game show; *The Celestine Prophecy*, a movie based on James Redfield's best-selling book; and *El Reto Final* for FOX Sports, Seasons 1, 2, and 3, a soccer reality series.

Web
Added
Value™

*Free value-added materials available from
the Download Resource Center at www.jrosspub.com*

At J. Ross Publishing we are committed to providing today's professional with practical, hands-on tools that enhance the learning experience and give readers an opportunity to apply what they have learned. That is why we offer ancillary materials available for download on this book and all participating Web Added Value™ publications. These online resources may include interactive versions of material that appears in the book or supplemental templates, worksheets, models, plans, case studies, proposals, spreadsheets and assessment tools, among other things. Whenever you see the WAV™ symbol in any of our publications it means bonus materials accompany the book and are available from the Web Added Value™ Download Resource Center at www.jrosspub.com.

Downloads available for *Branded Entertainment: Dealmaking Strategies and Techniques for Industry Professionals* include a sample term sheet, a sample Branded Entertainment agreement, and a PowerPoint presentation that explains what Branded Entertainment is to agencies, networks, and brands.

CHAPTER 1

Defining Branded Entertainment: What It Is and What It Is Not

Our media options have increased and evolved more in the last decade than over the last century. Think about that. We are living in times that call for constant change. Changes all around us are happening instantaneously. Changes are being experienced at a surface level but are impacting us collectively to the core. How we act, react, and consume mutates constantly.

How does constant change impact a brand? Today, a brand preserving the status quo is almost nonexistent. Brands are experiencing a process of evolution: riding a fast track and being forced into an express lane. The positioning of a brand within a tumultuous world of options is the new challenge. Today, the labyrinth of media options that a brand must consider requires a new order for action. This new order redefines when it makes the most sense to be "in" and for how long. The big question is whether to live inside or outside relevant content (yes, inside content that has been created with the brand in mind). The informed answer to that question hinges on having an understanding of Branded Entertainment (BE)—knowing what it is and what it is not.

WHAT BRANDED ENTERTAINMENT IS

Branded Entertainment Is a Solution to an Evolution

The evolution of our media options has revolutionized the way we view entertainment. Viewers want it all *now* and are no longer willing to wait—the immediate self-gratification syndrome. This syndrome can also be seen in the world of brands. Brands continuously evolve, faster than ever before, while more brands are coming into the market to compete. With so many options available at only a glance, consumers do not want to wait for results. If a brand does not deliver its promise on the spot, the brand can be immediately replaced—with no remorse.

Brand "doctors" now have to rethink ways to evolve along with technology. Media evolution does not only mean having more options to choose from—media evolution also means creating ways to be quick and react in a blink before being moved out of the game. Brands now understand this.

As the playing field evolves, messages to consumers need to be more refined and emotionally engaging. The delivery

OMNIPRESENCE

Figure 1.1. *Omnipresence*—the new keyword for a brand.

of a brand needs to be more personal. The delivery has to have an emotional rhythm that speaks to consumers. A more creative way to do this has to be in the works. New, creative delivery methods are to brands like cement is to a foundation. Not reacting to this new (marketing) world order exposes brand managers and networks alike to losing consumers' attention.

The consequences of slow evolution are simply concluded in one fact: consumers are less passive and more demanding regarding what suits their personal needs. A consumer no longer travels to content. Content must travel to the consumer. Therefore, *omnipresence* is the new keyword for a brand (Figure 1.1). A brand no longer holds center stage: it fluidly finds its way inside the social media world of consumers; it becomes part of a series drama; it is part of a song consumers cannot keep out of their heads.

Figure 1.2. Create outstanding branding content by cultivating brand participation and creative content simultaneously.

Branded Entertainment Stems from a Seed ... Timing Is Everything

When we think about marrying content with a brand, we rarely wonder who came to the party first. Was it an idea for content that came first and the brand was found later? Or was it the brand that was looking to expand into the content? Some would ask: why does that even matter? The truth is it does matter because how you start a creative process determines whether you finish it successfully. The key to creating outstanding branding content is to cultivate the brand and the content simultaneously (Figure 1.2).

There is a certain similarity in pairing branding with content creation to the germination of a tree sprouted from a seed. In creating content, the idea for the content (assuming there is a need) is the "seed" in this process. This seed should be grafted in its infancy to the story of a brand. Here, "infancy" is not the first creative impulse or the launch of a narrative arc. It is the moment when an idea that may potentially be targeted for a branded deal enters the picture. The key is to identify the moment and immediately begin looking for brands to partner with rather than to leave the brand out as a placeholder to be filled later. Because each brand has a story to be told, the unfolding of the story has to happen along with the development of the idea. To create a successful foundation for Branded Entertainment, the story of the brand within the content needs to unfold organically and alongside the content itself—the story must feel natural to the consumer; otherwise the message risks being ignored.

This creative mesh must continue refining itself and serving as the stage where the brand's story will live. The brand can then be like an actual character within the content: it has a purpose, a message, and a destination. The idea can then transform into engaging content as the development process unfolds. The trick is that both the content and the brand need to be set on "START" about the same time.

The opposite of this would be for a brand to participate in or be inserted into some content already in existence. At this point, most likely the brand would merely select from a branch of existing options within the content. Because the content is already fully formed, flexibility is often limited and as a result, a proper fit between brand and content is rare. We see this in sponsorship deals in which the brand associates with the content at the end of its creation, but the content did not have the brand in mind from its inception. The content may have been brought to you by a fine product, but the association between the two usually is not strong enough to leave a lasting impression. Ultimately this weakness will fail both the brand and the content. The failure, however, is more significant for the brand than for the content creators.

Some of the best examples of failing to mesh the brand and content from the beginning concern mass consumption brands. These brands often have tried to create new content with no "star power" or at times have pushed a product based

Figure 1.3. The soft-sell strategy: from the "ignition point," simultaneously develop Branded Entertainment content united with the brand without being obvious.

on a hard-sell approach instead of a soft sell—a sure recipe for disaster. Plucking product within content can be a serious turn off. In the past, cleaning product brands have fallen into this trap. Because their target is to reach a range of consumers as wide and vast as possible, some consumer cleaning product brands (due to their frequency of use and price point) must align with distributors and producers who can make outstanding popular and engaging content and not settle for anything less. If star power can be added to the mix, then instant recognition and an emotional connection are more attainable. Instead, too often, mass consumption brands go for the hard sell by making the product and its consumption too obvious (in your face) where it feels unnatural.

Branded Entertainment means content needs to be united to the brand from the "ignition point," at the same time, without being obvious (Figure 1.3). This technique is a soft sell strategy. Nowadays, brands are around only for short periods of time. Some even say their time on the shelf is "predestined." Others say "mutate often" in order to survive.

Destiny, however, can be altered when we understand how to become part of a new game. Be an agent of change, not of extinction. New formulas of brand + content exist. More and more they need to be the *new formula* inside a media strategy.

A word of caution: Any type of branded content to be created, short- or long-form, must first and foremost fulfill a gap, a visible need in the viewers' world. Consider this concept to be a "universal law" in the world of Branded Entertainment. Once the new content finds a place within the landscape of consumers, viewers will tend to multiply awareness to others faster than any marketing campaign could. In other words, when consumers feel heard and a brand comes in to fulfill a dream, a wish, or an emotional engagement for a viewer, the viewer will become a carrier of the brand's message. This scenario can be considered to be branded content success.

Remember the movie *You've Got Mail?* Who doesn't remember that this flick jump-started the process of online dating? It brought home the concept of intertwining emotions with good marketing. Even the title was a homerun, linking the brand's core message to a personal sensation evoked in any consumer.

Branded Entertainment Is an Independent Island

Branded Entertainment deals must live in a "Switzerland" of media and brands—the nature of being neutral to all parties no matter what. Earlier the idea of branded content was compared to a seedling that turns into the soul or essence of a project. If this idea holds true by delivering to viewers what they want while the brand is properly represented, then the deal will be healthy and have a strong foundation for success. This strong foundation needs to grow on independent ground, meaning that the idea ultimately brings together the pillars of media: agencies, networks/media outlets, and producers. The goal of these "newborn" deals, known as Branded Entertainment deals, is to support business inside this trinity and to encourage new ways to assemble deals among them: *freedom with independence!*

What happens if this freedom and independence are not part of the foundation? What happens if instead an idea is born from:

- Pressure to make cheaper content
- Pressure to generate new business because of a shrinking 30-second advertisement world
- A lack of funding to get an idea sold

In these situations, the seedling idea may grow fast, but it may also perish at the first sign of a storm or a drought. What we truly seek in Branded Entertainment is longevity for content that now nurtures a brand inside it. Branded Entertainment is about allowing, not constricting. When freedom is allowed, chances are the lifespan of a concept will last more than a season.

Branded Entertainment = Emotional Connection

Who really knows what Branded Entertainment is? One clue to finding useful sources of information on the subject is to ask experts. These "experts" usually understand what it means to be emotionally connected to something.

Establishing an emotional connection is a goal in itself. When a brand reaches a point that is intertwined to consumers' emotions, we know it has "arrived."

The same principle applies to content. When a show, a series, or a character inhabits the lives of viewers and is recalled or identified as part of who they are, that is when we know a connection has been made.

Many in this business ask: how long does it take for a brand to see results in a Branded Entertainment deal? Usually a brand has to execute a full "first season" of content on the air to properly interpret the experience of consumers and the type of emotional attachment felt about the newly created Branded Entertainment content. Basically, after a full season has aired, a brand can start to measure results.

What Branded Entertainment seeks is a long-term emotional connection. If the brand is *in*, then the mission is accomplished. An *in-love* experience, better known as an "emotional bond," creates a monogamous relationship. In these days of "intense affairs," failing to reach monogamous status is a luxury brand managers cannot afford (Figure 1.4).

WHAT BRANDED ENTERTAINMENT IS NOT

Branded Entertainment Is Not Product Placement

To understand Branded Entertainment, product placement, what it is and how it came to be, needs further explanation. The origins of product placement date back to the first days of television. Back then, networks were looking to find solutions for integrating brands that wanted in on the business of reaching the masses. In return, these brands offered cash to fund the big shows.

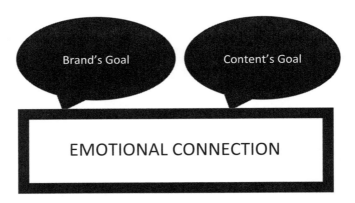

Figure 1.4. Branded Entertainment seeks an emotional connection between the content and the brand that can lead to a long-term "monogamous" relationship.

Long before the idea to generate 30-second commercials came to be, the networks found ways to integrate brands "inside" TV shows. A brand was placed inside the show in a static form. The logo and packaging of the product were visible to viewers who then became exposed and aware of the existence of that brand.

In more advanced examples, brand jingles were catchy enough that they played a role in the euphoria of a TV program audience. Back then, many shows were taped in front of live audiences. Jingles were turned into useful tools to create collective excitement for a network show, thus bringing a brand to recognition. It did not matter if the brand shared any relevance to the content of the show. Detergents were some of the first brands that took advantage of this boom and were the origin of the term "soap operas."

Later, the emergence of commercials gave birth to the industry of advertising. Now brands could take time to tell their stories, their way, in a manner that captivated the consumer. After all, the thinking was why have partial retention from viewers *inside* a show when the brand could have full retention *in between* shows?

And so it was. The story continued to evolve with the two industries living side-by-side, growing and making money off each other for over a half century until technology opened the gateway for viewers to be more entertained with fewer interruptions.

With a shrinking viewer pie, lower ratings, and more options for niche channels to choose from, the networks decided to invite big brands into a show to be a partner from within. Brands were willing to put bigger dollars on the table if their media buy was enhanced by some form of brand presence within the content. This partnering was more like an association. Today most people know this type of association as *product placement*—invited back into the fold as a quick response to the diminishing commercial ad viewing patterns.

How, then, is Branded Entertainment differentiated from what we know product placement to be? Can a clear definition distinguishing the two be created? Yes, with three words: *alive*, *organic*, and *seamless* (Figure 1.5).

Alive. In a Branded Entertainment model, a brand no longer has a passive status. What makes a brand "alive" are its attributes coming to life within the content, sometimes to the extent of ignoring the brand's name in its entirety. Whatever that brand's story stands for, it stands side-by-side and on equal grounds with the content itself. Its "activation in motion" is what makes a brand alive. All this means activating a brand's purpose and intertwining with the characters and the plot of the content in a way that makes sense,

BRANDED
ENTERTAINMENT

ALIVE

ORGANIC

SEAMLESS

Figure 1.5. Branded Entertainment is differentiated from product place-ment by three words: alive, organic, and seamless.

entertains, and remains true to all. For example, a GPS from a known automotive brand ends up resolving the mystery of a murder within a plot. With no obvious mention of the car brand or a visual shot of the car's logo, the functionality of the GPS creates an immediate emotional engagement for the viewer and the brand's best use of its attributes.

Organic. The term "organic" often signifies "no chemical additives." In the Branded Entertainment industry, "organic" means the brand and the content created are a "natural mar-riage," enhancing the nature of power and not force. When something is created with the purpose to unite, power is created. When two things are put together, just because they need to be together, a forceful "marriage" is made. This dif-ference of power versus force is real and makes a difference between short-lived and long-lived deals. In a natural mar-riage, the content and the brand are part of the same creation. The relationship cannot feel unnatural, forced, or tainted.

The viewer should see and get the message without the message seeming forced in any way. For example, an Android phone becomes the carrier of clues in a reality competition. Each clue can be further figured out by the best use of this mobile device's features.

Seamless. When the lines become truly blurred, and defragmenting the brand from the story is impossible, only then can the term "seamless" be applied. Content creators can only succeed in attaining "seamless" when they understand the brand initiatives at a visceral level and have made them part of the content's DNA. As simple as these words sound, time is required to decode the purpose and attributes of a brand. Only when the purpose and the attributes of a brand are understood can content be created with an integrated "chip" that will incorporate these moments seamlessly so the brand and the show seem like one. For example, a home improvement show features some smart ways to remodel a home. The tools and products used in the show are all about "ease of use." This is the same message the particular home improvement retailer's brand represents. To a viewer, remodeling in simple, smart ways and going to this do-it-yourself retailer to execute an idea seem like one and the same.

Branded Entertainment Is Not the "Pac-Man" of the 30-Second Commercial World

This concept is probably one of the most controversial and argued points in the multimedia industry. A media strategy aims to expose key messages to a particular audience in a particular frequency of time. The strategy embeds a goal and seeks quantitative results. Most of the confusion derives from the flawed understanding that media and

Branded Entertainment work against each other in a zero-sum dynamic.

This erroneous belief stems primarily from budgetary reasons. When monies are taken away from media to be allocated to a branded solution, many consider it to be a cannibalistic decision and fail to see its complimentary value, sort of like Pac-Man eating all the pellets in the video game.

Nowadays it is more accurate to say that budgets are a "work in progress." At this competitive stage of brands and survival, we are starting to see "vanguardist" brands, or brands at the forefront of the industry, separate their dollars to supply both initiatives: media and entertainment solutions. The key here is to educate the top decision makers. At the brand level, decision makers must clearly understand that a media buy with integrations inside content is a combination intended to enhance the brand experience to the consumer so that brand managers in turn can formulate ways to apply both strategies to execute them as an undivided solution.

Branded Entertainment is more subtle than media. Its compounding effects, when done properly, can only enhance and increase the overall value of a media strategy. Branded Entertainment must be seen as a complement to a media strategy, not as a hungry force unleashed to devour the advertising industry.

A Branded Entertainment Solution Is Not a Sub of the Whole—It Is the Whole

Broadcasters, cable networks, and social media are all looking to take a bigger piece of the pie—the viewers' attention pie. Unfortunately, viewing patterns are not growing as fast as new options. Branded Entertainment is mistakenly seen as a solution born to live under soon-to-be-obsolete strategies. Branded Entertainment is not viewed in its totality, so let's review it from a media outlet perspective.

When a network proposes the creation of a new sub-internal division called *Client Solutions*, the solutions are often compromised by internal agendas born from the traditional ad sales and programming departments. The motive is to attract those dollars (now endangered, according to them) back home where they belong. This is not a client-focused strategy—what brands and clients are looking for on a long-term basis.

The problem here is that creative measures are just merely tactics to attach existing content to certain brands with the only true goal being to bring in more ad revenue. This attachment is forced and will be unconsciously rejected by consumers.

The result is a short-term sale. Clients may buy into it for one cycle, but the short lifespan of these ideas comes to a quick end when not properly executed. The result is only a short-term win that does not live up to expectations in a second cycle or season.

This approach remains questionable and short sighted when looked at from the point of view of a traditional ad agency. Why? It starts with the motive.

Ad agencies are a breed in constant mutation. As their core and traditional business model continues to diminish, the idea to bring in entertaining content in the form of a "disguised ad" seems to be a quick solution for survival. In addition, the brands that comprise the agency's roster of clients are less bound by the sort of loyalty that once held those relationships in place. This situation is shrinking ad and creative groups, forcing them to become more fragmented, more competitive, and ultimately causing their agencies to operate in survival mode. The best long-term business decisions are rarely made when survival is at stake.

Problems arise when a traditional ad agency shortcuts a desperately needed creative process and instead only uses an elongated version of the story of a traditional commercial. Even worse, using this approach can kill an idea before it is born to protect the traditional business model, which is currently in intensive care.

The result? A train headed for a wreck. Practices on Branded Entertainment solutions need to be in the new "book" for these agencies. Agencies are still are quite valuable to the new process of developing content for brands.

Branded Entertainment Is Not a Longer Version of a 30-Second Ad Campaign

Branded Entertainment content is created with the intention of *complementing* the efforts of an ad media campaign. The word "complementing," however, does not mean "to lengthen what already exists." An ad campaign serves a very specific purpose: it exists to convey a very particular message about a brand and its attributes. Every angle of creativity for the ad campaign only exists to support the effective delivery of that message.

Any attempt to transplant that creativity into entertainment content deflates the impact and can even turn consumers off. Once they feel the sale is "obvious," the results for a brand could be fatal. Ad agencies and creative shops must be vigilant to not interfere with a complementary idea that serves as an enhancer to an already existing media effort.

BRANDED ENTERTAINMENT MUST UNDERSTAND FIRST WHAT MEDIA SEEKS TO ACCOMPLISH

Emotional engagement is the goal.

Figure 1.6. Emotional engagement is the goal of Branded Entertainment concepts.

Branded Entertainment content must first seek to understand what the media part of a deal wants to accomplish. Then, the creative content should incorporate that understanding into an entirely different creative product that suits a bigger entertainment-driven goal. Emotional engagement is the goal for Branded Entertainment concepts (Figure 1.6).

WHY BRANDED ENTERTAINMENT NOW?

Technological advances are now part of the overall restructuring formula of media consumption. Media outlets can truly identify who and what viewers are consuming. So there is no more guessing and no more wasting of media dollars on consumers who are not a target. Microscopically speaking, brand leaders and networks now know which consumer is the real buying consumer. Ad time between programs is becoming increasingly less relevant to viewers, especially when new technologies offer an ideal alternative: downloading, fast forwarding, and recording content. In other words, consumers now view content on their own terms when they want it. Ads are being ignored.

Continuous development in technology has given all of the power to consumers. If they don't have to wait, they won't. Immediate gratification is what consumers look for; the tables have turned. Once upon a time, consumers had to look for content. Now content has to travel to consumers. So where does that leave all the media campaigns aimed at living in the "in between-program" world?

Just as technology has evolved in stages, so will brand media campaigns have to alter their basic form and expression, mutating inside a new world of consumerism. This is why *the now* is *now*. The future is here—all blends, all flows as one (or maybe we are going back to the old ways when TV started and brands were the platform stage for content and content would have not existed without brands).

Branded Entertainment's time is *now* because we are dealing with a compounding reality that is not going away. Viewers have more choices of content and more platforms for viewing this content than ever before. Branded Entertainment creates a "back-door solution" to the leaking effect brands are experiencing in regard to the numbers of eyeballs dropping out of mass platforms.

All of the traditional cost-per-thousand investment models are in need of drastic change. The solution does not come out of lowering the price as the eyeball levels equally drop. The emergence of a new solution would recalibrate the investment ratio of brand versus airtime. It would now measure the direct impact a brand has on viewers as the brand is brought to life within engaging content that viewers cannot live without. This emergence of a new business model invokes the presence of an effective Branded Entertainment team inclusive of agencies and media outlets. (We will explore later how the contribution of an effective, inclusive Branded Entertainment team can support the process without any of the players taking possession of the entire formula.)

WHY NOT IMPLEMENT BRANDED ENTERTAINMENT "DOWN THE ROAD?"

The recent economic downturn has convinced many companies that embracing "anorexia" is a "safe play." In doing so, the thinking of these companies is that by cutting personnel, the savings generated will lead them out of the present tension. The gamble here is that cutting resources previously charged with finding innovative ways to reach consumers will not result in their brands losing what they had already gained in better times. Unfortunately for many companies, the truth is that by standing still these companies are losing ground. History shows that in times of uncertainty and economic crisis, innovative breakthroughs have occurred time and time again. Necessity is truly the mother of invention. When the status quo gets broken, it opens up a door of opportunity where rebuilding and rethinking are possible and new growth can emerge. By rethinking the possibilities, it is then possible to use tough times to adapt and reformulate new strategies and make them the new standard. This is where Branded Entertainment deals come into the picture. *Important*: Remain vigilant against "corporate anorexia" that leads us all down a path of self-annihilation.

The next wave of evolution is the reinvention of formulas, the recalibration of value, and the repurposing of each player

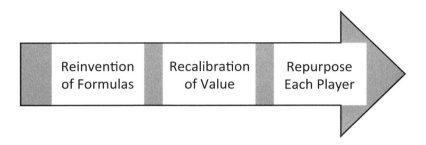

Figure 1.7. The next wave of evolution in Branded Entertainment: working together to reinvent the formulas, recalibrate the values, repurpose the roles of players in the media/consumer game, and to reach new goal and skill levels.

in the media/consumer game (Figure 1.7). We all can manage to stay in the game—by playing together—but our goals and skills need to reach new levels.

Raising skillsets to new levels and reformulating the value of a business are not always the hardest parts of this process. Usually, what takes up more time and effort is the resistance to change. It seems like we are all born with resistance—almost as if resistance is a natural human condition. Corporations behave very much like humans. They like formulas because formulas create processes and systems. They enjoy implementing formulas because little thinking is required. So, when the formulas have to be recalibrated or even recreated, people will automatically be impacted negatively by this shift. In some way, our natural resistance opposes the way to change.

Too much too soon has already happened all around us. No one can deny the tremendous impact technology has had on all of us over the last decade. Even our brains have been

reprogrammed to think differently because our way of pro-
cessing information has been in a constant state of flux. This
is nature's way of letting us know nothing ever stays the same.

Change is now here. There is no point in delaying the
obvious. By trying to keep serving an old, dying system, more
threat will come out of attempting to survive than accepting
change itself. Once this concept is accepted, the *new* will start
to emerge and *new ways* will begin to surface, collectively
impacting industry and establishing a new standard. Do not
be paralyzed by fear. Stop hiding under the excuse of a weak
economy. Realize that a new paradigm is always an opportunity for new roles and titles to emerge. New leaders will rise.
Be a leader in Branded Entertainment. Do not fight Branded
Entertainment just because it is new. Embrace it. Enjoy being
out of your comfort zone. Soon enough, you will feel comfortable again.

CHAPTER 2

Two Words, One New Approach: Branded Entertainment

Most go-getters in the media industry have a positive reaction to the term *Branded Entertainment*. They immediately associate the term with money and trends, but the next thing they ask is "Can it happen?" The short answer is "Yes," but the truth is that most people do not really understand *how* a deal in Branded Entertainment is assembled.

Unraveling the mysteries surrounding three questions can help networks, content producers, and brand managers to understand how Branded Entertainment deals come to life. Answering these three questions is the first step to

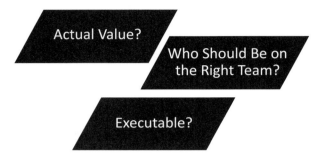

Figure 2.1. A Branded Entertainment deal needs answers to three key questions: what is the value, who is on the team, and will the execution work.

comprehending the practice in a simpler fashion and embracing how Branded Entertainment is different from product placement. A basic understanding of what Branded Entertainment deals are and who jump-starts the process will be covered next. In this chapter and in the chapters that follow, how the answers to each of these questions become an intrinsic part in an actual deal will be discussed (Figure 2.1):

- Question 1: What is the actual value of a deal and what is it worth to a brand?
- Question 2: Who should be on the "right" team to assemble the deal? (The entire assembly includes the proposition, the execution, and the delivery.)
- Question 3: Can execution of a Branded Entertainment deal work?

WHAT IS THE ACTUAL VALUE OF A DEAL AND WHAT IS IT WORTH TO A BRAND?

Brands are all about negotiating valuations. Brand managers are used to dealing with seconds of airtime and eyeballs of consumers. They like to view a deal in cost per thousand terminology. Brand managers also like to have a base—a point of reference, a past experience, or a competitor's case study that proves that their deal has similar value. What is so intimidating about a deal of this nature is that these known valuations are only to be used as *references* to traditional commercial deals. They do not represent the true value of a Branded Entertainment deal.

The first consideration is to know what a Branded Entertainment deal of this type could bring to the table. The thing to keep in mind here is that a deal's worth is not necessarily measured solely in financial terms, which may cause some angst in the beginning. You may hear things such as, "If you can't show me that the money (value) is there, then why should I bother with a Branded Entertainment deal?" Money absolutely matters in Branded Entertainment deals, but the money usually comes as the result of *fulfilling a primary purpose central to the brand itself.* Examples of primary purposes that can drive revenue when addressed by a successful deal include:

- Is the brand being confused with other similar brands?
- Is the brand's aura not letting consumers evaluate the superior features of the product?

One of the main mysteries in Branded Entertainment deals is that a brand manager has to first see the primary purpose in what a Branded Entertainment deal seeks to accomplish. Rather than just being one more message in the space of consumers, the brand should aim at being "the sun" to its consumers. Once this primary reason is central to the brand leaders, then the second consideration of determining a monetary value can be reached.

Multiple examples of how to measure the worth and value of a deal will be covered in Chapters 5 and 6, but for now, in simple terms, a combination of formulas can be created. For instance, a portion of the deal can be measured based on the reach the deal will have on the platforms where the content will live. Another portion of the deal can be measured based on the notion that the content can be leased or owned depending on the nature of the deal. If owned, a licensing fee may be part of the formula.

WHO SHOULD BE ON THE RIGHT TEAM TO ASSEMBLE THE DEAL: THE PROPOSITION, THE EXECUTION, AND THE DELIVERY

The mystery surrounding "who should be on the right team" is an important issue to resolve. Team membership is a great differentiating point between an ad/commercial deal and a pure content deal. The primary reason for this differentiation is that in Branded Entertainment deals, multiple constituencies come to the table to speak about the creative process, procedures, reach, and the multiplying effect to consumers, among other things. Not only are multiple constituencies from one platform or from the brand present, but representatives from the producers and possibly the agency who may understand how to package it all into one are also present.

Whereas a deal moves from one place to another in a sequential form in traditional settings, in Branded Entertainment deals, we want to maintain a high level of participation from multiple parties, at parallel times, with all aiming to reach our goals at once. Achieving our goals and having simultaneous participation are by no means easy, but this process is far more engaging and lively than any of the current (dying) traditional formulas.

The key element is to appoint a champion who is willing to move the project through to completion, not in a linear form, but simultaneously, involving all parties in the deal at numerous times during the project's lifecycle. The nature of a Branded Entertainment deal can be compared to the nature of time. The passage of time may appear to be linear, but it really is not. All things in nature happen simultaneously.

Where should the champion come from: the agency, the platform/network, or the production company (e.g., the producer who is closest to the content)? This is a good question. The answer is: *it depends*. As will be explored later in greater detail, Branded Entertainment deals should have a leading party. The champion/leader can be the agency, a producer, or a network. In practice, however, the champion usually comes from the party who ignites the idea and brings it to the table with the intention of moving the idea into a deal.

CAN THE EXECUTION OF A BRANDED ENTERTAINMENT DEAL WORK?

The current lack of established sources that can easily measure the impact of Branded Entertainment is one main reason why Branded Entertainment deals are not yet abundant in the industry. There is a natural sense of rejection when the results of a deal cannot be measured in quantitative terms.

This situation can be compared to the common problem of the chicken and the egg. Resources cannot be invested in measuring results until there is enough business to measure, but the explosion of more Branded Entertainment deals cannot happen until measuring tools are in place.

The question here is about execution. Can the execution of a Branded Entertainment deal work? The answer is "Yes, it can."

To circumvent the lack of established sources to easily measure the impact of Branded Entertainment, some brands want to pioneer this new way of thinking. A handful of companies are willing to measure the potential impact of Branded Entertainment across a particular group of consumers. These companies are starting to measure the impact of highly powerful content as opposed to new content.

To measure impact, some organizations are creating methods for postresearch analysis that focus more on the qualitative impact a deal may have had on a group of consumers. Brands are quite savvy in this area. Well-organized brands have small teams within their organizations that perform studies to test a brand for a potential market launch. Usually these teams select a test market, a microscopic universe, representative of what the rest of the country or the world might do, and use that market as a sample group to measure reactions and the likelihood of purchase of the product. A similar practice can be replicated to measure the impact of branded content. This practice carries an investment, but what can be learned from the results can be impactful to the success and growth of a brand.

Social media is another avenue to use, not only to try to measure the success of the branded content, but also to grow the brand's message within a target audience. If a platform already exists wherein brands can speak directly to consumers, imagine if the audience could now engage with actual talent or characters from a series they love. How much more would they be willing to tell you? When these consumers begin to bond and communicate with all that is relatable, and if the content has strong engagement, then chances are the measurement of results will also be attached to that organic relationship.

If, however, a platform does not yet exist or the platform has had little development, then a branded deal could serve as the launching pad for a "heavenly space" where your consumers can come to you and you can go to them for information, any day at anytime. Now, is that not the Holy Grail everyone is searching for?

MISUSING BRANDED ENTERTAINMENT

Currently, when Branded Entertainment is discussed as a new opportunity, depending on who is having the conversation, one of three very common scenarios usually follows. In each case, these scenarios often look more like a way out of trouble than an approach to doing business in a different way.

Common Perspectives

Some of the quick-fix Branded Entertainment scenarios that are presently missing the bigger picture, as seen from their respective perspectives, include:

- A brand manager: *Our brand has found a way into desirable content.* Perhaps, but is this situation creating a real shift for the brand? Consider this frequent scenario. A serial show becomes a hit, and brands want to be part of that success no matter what. For instance, when talent search shows were hitting big rating numbers and capturing instant success, consumer product brands with power had to get a piece of the action, even if it only meant having a glass with their logo on the table of the show's celebrity judges. Achieving the presence of the brand on the show was accomplished, but did it really create a significant shift?

- A content producer: *How are we going to get the series off the ground? We need a brand!* The content has a chance to be produced only because of a brand's investment, but is there real creativity put toward the inclusion of the brand into the preconceived content? This situation is the old fashioned scenario in which the idea for a show/series gets green-lit and then funding has to be raised to have the show/series produced. Most prime-time shows on the top networks were born from this foundation. The level of creativity was limited for the brand and most times the execution was only seen as logo presence on the screen as a billboard or bumper in/out of commercials. The goal to reach a particular number of consumers may be reached, but is this goal good enough to create a personality for the brand?

- An agency: *Branded Entertainment definitely sounds innovative enough to keep our agency's billing growing.* Has creative work been done to think through how the brand will really fit in? In the case of an online series, created solely by the brand's agency, the brand is well positioned in each webisode, but is the content of the webisode good enough to create a viral following and true consumer engagement? Health and beauty brands have often taken this approach in search of in-content participation, but in doing so did the approach create a real shift for the brand? Most importantly, have the webisodes really been watched by a wide enough audience to make a real impact? Brands in these categories, soaps in particular, benefit from large mass consumption given that the product's price point is low and usage is high.

In each of these examples, Branded Entertainment is mostly viewed as a *solution* to a problem, not as a *new approach* to doing business. Branded Entertainment is looked at as more of an immediate problem solver. Now you are probably wondering: what's wrong with that? Well, immediate solutions have a tendency to die young. When Branded Entertainment emerges as a simple solution to common media problems, the engagement process gets shortened, corners are cut, and as a result the goals of the other parties in the deal tend to be ignored. This is where problems begin. Now you have a new set of obstacles to overcome rather than a truly new approach.

The "quick-fix" misconception misses the mark because it fails to fully appreciate the concept being put in motion as a complete business methodology. That said, as we look at

Figure 2.2. In addition to being a potential problem solver for agencies and brands, Branded Entertainment is also a new trend, an alternative approach to current advertising, and a new version of product placement.

the various ways Branded Entertainment is understood, or partially understood, in the industry, a three-dimensional image is beginning to emerge from the many observed sides. In addition to having the potential to solve problems, as shown in Figure 2.2, Branded Entertainment is also:

- A "cool" trend with added cache for those who can seamlessly pull it off
- An alternative approach to brands that have grown bored with 30-second ads
- Version 2.0 of product placement

What does this really mean?

Cool. Industry insiders who view Branded Entertainment as "cool" are latching onto it because they see Branded Entertainment as both new and innovative. Branded

Entertainment reflects modern thinking for the brands and an unexplored way to get to consumers.

An alternative approach. Recognizing Branded Entertainment as an alternative approach implies an acceptance of the concept that brands have options to choose from. Brands can create content beyond the traditional 30-second spot. A brand can opt in on ideas for entertaining content and play an integral role in the development of the content.

Product Placement Version 2.0. Ultimately, embracing Branded Entertainment as "Product Placement 2.0" reveals an understanding that content and brands can now live side-by-side—the brand is no longer relegated to the background. The 2.0 upgrade specifically refers to the potential of Branded Entertainment to create a more even relationship between the content and the brand.

Obstacles

Creating balanced relationships in which content and brands are positioned on an equal level is the goal for both getting a deal done and having the end product considered a success for all involved. The obstacles for each of the primary players involved in getting this goal—producers, media outlets, and the brands themselves—all primarily stem from misinterpretations.

The content producers. Content producers most often see Branded Entertainment as nothing more than a better way to get funding for either a project or a series. Content producers see a side-step around the traditional pitching process that leads to a much faster pathway to approval. Rather than having to wait in line for approval of a typical proposal by which the media outlet is the sole source of funding, the content producer sees the Branded Entertainment project as one that will stand out for its creative structuring and from there on stand on its own unique merits. Bringing brand support to the table creates a much sexier proposition that enables freedom and with it greater content creativity—every producer's dream! Of course, any notion of near-absolute independence on the production side inherently excludes contributions other than those of the monetary variety from the very brand that is helping to make all of this happen.

The media. Not only is there the not-so-little matter of including the voice of the brand in the co-produced Branded Entertainment venture, but there is also the current challenge of landing the pitch: if the dynamics of Branded Entertainment are not effectively communicated, the media outlets on the receiving end of the pitch may dismiss Branded Entertainment as being too risky or complicated. More often than not, the media outlet either cannot see the benefit (because the benefit has not been clearly defined) or does not know how to gauge its effectiveness. The media will come back to the producer and say, "It's interesting, but we're still not quite sure how it works for us." Just as challenging is when such a deal is dismissed as being too complicated, more often than not because previous experiences have suggested to the outlet that the necessary coordination involved will be a nightmare.

The brands. What about the brands? Brands are no longer getting the same return out of traditional advertising alone. The results boil down to eyeballs. Content is now being watched when consumers want to, not when they have to—a big change. The commercials that used to accompany such content are being deleted or fast-forwarded past all the time. Brands see the potential benefits of Branded Entertainment and would like to toy around with the idea, but who can lead them to the "promised land?" Is the agency representing a brand able to see all sides of the picture to help guide the process and even temper expectations if necessary?

What makes Branded Entertainment so unique as a concept and a media offering is that Branded Entertainment has the potential to be a panacea for all parties involved. Branded Entertainment does not seek to put one solution above all others but to accomplish several goals at once. So, is it really that simple? Of course not. Anytime you attempt to offer this type of panacea solution, the task is not an easy one to accomplish, but it is certainly worth going down this road.

MAKING BRANDED ENTERTAINMENT

To avoid falling into the common mistake of *using* Branded Entertainment rather than *making* Branded Entertainment, I reiterate time and time again to really be clear in the understanding of what this concept of Branded Entertainment is.

Using. Using Branded Entertainment translates into not thinking through thoroughly how all the parts fit in from the start. For example, a content idea seems ideal to a media platform; whoever can produce the content idea cheaper gets to do it; and at the end, a brand is needed to offset the cost of the production. No major thinking is required here.

Making. Making Branded Entertainment is about putting the parties together from the start of the deal, meaning that prior to a content idea the brand has to be at the table ready to make a Branded Entertainment venture happen. For example, the brand wants to differentiate itself from other competitors in its category. The brand wants to transcend into a content idea. The network has a need to shift toward a different type of content at a particular time. The agency sees the potential to walk the client into this new territory. All throughout, the process is rather proactive and creative—that is the difference.

Let me share a bit at this point from the case study discussed at the end of this book. The case concerns a brand that wanted to be engaged from the start in the comeback of a sports car model that once upon a time had been "the cool vehicle to drive." As relaunched years later, this brand asked for true creativity within the plot of a show—and so it was. The main star of the series was a soccer player on the rise. In the first episode, the owner of the top soccer club in the country wanted the soccer star to play on his team. The owner gave the soccer star the car as a gift. Drama was high throughout the episode, but the presentation of the gift, a convertible no less, provided a temporary break from the ongoing tension. The key to the car was delivered in a peculiar gift box. When the star opened it, he ran to look down from the balcony and saw a "ready for action" toy. If there was any question in viewers' minds as to what "the cool vehicle to drive" was, the star's face and the urgency he displayed in wanting to get behind the wheel answered it. At the end of the segment, we see the director's shot from above as the convertible drives off at high speed and hear the main character screaming from the top of his lungs, "Yes!"

Brands, producers, and agencies are all looking to not only survive, but to also stay on top of what is new and innovative. Achieving the goals of all parties involved as the overall result translates into long-term success for a Branded Entertainment joint venture. If everyone gets something out of this newly formed relationship, chances are this solution could work for the long haul. Is that not what all parties in the media industry are searching for?

Branded Entertainment has emerged as a new solution— a way to keep up with the pace and a new medium to enable communication between companies and consumers. This solution only requires leadership in orchestrating the parties in the right way so that the brands, media outlets, and agencies have a new way to do more business together.

How do we align these constituencies to have a parallel understanding of a bigger playground where we can all manage to stay in the game and play together? The way to unite the constituencies is by assembling a plan that involves each of their interests and goals—what Branded Entertainment really tries to accomplish.

So simple, right?

Easier said than done.

MAKING BRANDED ENTERTAINMENT INTO A DEAL

Brands evolve in very much the same way as consumers do. Certain brand teams have an inherent vision that allows them to see what the next trend might be. These are the brands that most welcome Branded Entertainment ventures. For instance, emerging brands such as technology-based services and wireless device companies tend to be confident in their media solutions and have an insatiable appetite for the next frontier. These emerging brands are not satisfied with the status quo. They are *naturals*—pioneers within their own categories. There is inherent understanding among trailblazers that content is king and, more importantly, that content can be used as a multiplying factor to deliver benefits to a brand. It is the sharing of this understanding by all parties involved that gives us a starting point where we can start to actually make things happen.

With the common misconceptions now on the table, clearly each party must move beyond its own self-centered viewpoints and see the larger picture to appreciate the purpose and benefits of brands and media outlets working together. To redefine the old roles and assemble a viable Branded Entertainment proposition, three must-have components are:

- The right idea
- The right team
- The right agreement

Each of these components will be introduced in this section. They will be explored in greater detail in Chapter 4.

The Right Idea

Any idea has a better chance to succeed if it sources from a need. For our purposes, the idea in question hinges on a need in the consumer world related to entertainment. Where is the space where something may be lacking? What is missing in the big pie of possibilities? Are any areas being overlooked by other media outlets? Are any target groups being ignored or underserved? Ask these questions *before* attempting to think of what the idea ought to be—they may trigger insight.

Once we get glimpses of the gaps, we can then engage in a brainstorming session that will allow us to move freely and without barriers through the collective thinking and idea-generation process. What is the idea and its basic premise? Once determined, test the idea with a few trusted people in very simple terms. Check for any "holes" you may have missed. Adjust the idea if needed and find a sentence that describes the idea as simply as possible. Simple is good at the idea stage, but simple is not always easy to get to.

A simple idea, driven by need, will lead to a content idea (CI). The content idea will carry two things:

- Thoughts on content that can be developed to serve the need for consumers and capture them emotionally
- A brand attached to it that can participate in a pro-active way

The Right Team

A team is only as good as the skills of its members. At all levels, ideas are created, but that does not automatically mean that a team can develop an idea into a deal. Additionally, a deal cannot be fully created and executed by a single individual or by one entity without the support and interaction of others—another universal law in Branded Entertainment. Therefore, a team is assembled with members from each participating party who have unique sets of skills and clearly defined roles. The team must come together to develop an idea, along with the brand, and execute it with all the appropriate media sources. Once an idea turns into a potential deal, all parties participate by creating the team which will bring the deal to fruition.

Note: Chapter 4 will provide a more in-depth explanation of putting together a Branded Entertainment team. A Branded Entertainment team is a combination of people gathered from the parties interested in assembling a Branded Entertainment deal. The team's participants should include representatives from the brand leading the deal, the network/ delivery platform, the production group, and the agency/ mediator to provide a sound foundation for the Branded Entertainment team. Chapter 4 will also focus on the specific titles of the team participants.

The two most important skills to possess when participating on a Branded Entertainment team are production know-how and the ability to understand a brand's internal functioning. Achieving this co-existence of skills is true team success—success that can be found when individual skills are paired up in the right mix to produce the desired results. A mix of individuals who share similarities and complement one another in their set of base knowledge is what makes a team unique. The size of a deal may vary, but in my experience, a team of three individuals to put the deal in place is ideal: a creative, a decoder, and an implementer.

A creative. A creative content leader is tasked with the goal of fleshing out ideas and deliberating among a group of these ideas until one appears to fulfill the brand's objectives while also remaining entertaining to viewers, thus being able to also fulfill the network's objectives. For instance, *The Voice* was a show that elevated the awareness of a network instantly. *Sprint* was the brand that joined in the early days of the series. *Sprint* helped the network fulfill its objective of creating an immediate viral campaign. People were voting, commenting on the participants, and even purchasing songs through the *Sprint Network*.

A decoder. Once an idea comes to life, the second member, the decoder, will create a process for the brand to find all the touch points where the brand connects with each viewer. The decoder understands the ratio between creativity and financial parameters and ideally should come with an agency background.

An implementer. The implementer must ensure that there is viability and support to create marketing "noise" and awareness for the branded content. An individual with a media background from multiple media outlets is ideal for this role.

The right team has to be assembled, prepared, and equipped to serve the needs of a Branded Entertainment deal within the universe of content possibilities. This team must possess experience in creating content (short and long) and be able to formulate ideas that identify where content gaps might be in the industry—like those described above. When assembling a team, try to keep things colorful by having a variety of minds with multiple viewpoints present. That said, be sure the team is small and efficient. This is accomplished by asking (and answering) one key question of each participant: "Could this deal still happen if [this person] were not participating in the core team?" If the answer is "Yes," then you probably need to leave that person out of the inner mix of the deal.

The Right Agreement

If you have the impression that Branded Entertainment seems to be a very subjective process, well, the many shades of gray are about to get even more distinct. When it comes to agreeing to everything on paper, the right agreement is subject to the conditions from which the deal was born.

The notion of subjectivity suggests there are no clear-cut black and white answers to the many variables that will be encountered—but not because so many variables have been thrown into the mix. In the world of Branded Entertainment, no two deals are exactly alike. A Branded Entertainment deal is not the same as selling 30-second ads (although some people may say Branded Entertainment deals are only longer versions of ads). At the very core of branded transactions, each deal has a very specific purpose for each of the participants—and that makes each agreement unique.

At this early stage of the game, however, one should understand that often multiple agreements are needed to conclude a deal in Branded Entertainment. An umbrella agreement may not be enough, or even appropriate, to cover all the details of a multiple-party transaction. A one-agreement scenario is usually not ideal because it:

- May not be enough to fully protect all parties involved
- May lengthen the approval process because each party will have the right to change too many areas that from their point of view look "too gray"
- May need to stipulate dollars and cents when all parties do not need to know that degree of detail

- May very well be part of a larger transaction and confidentiality could be broken if shared with all parties
- May not address the trust factor for some parties (Some parties now linked by this transaction may never have done business together before; therefore, the trust factor plays a significant role for these parties—one very important reason why having more than one agreement makes sense.)
- May be unnecessary for some parties (Some partners may do business regularly so extending or amending an agreement already in place may be the way to go in creating this new deal.)

Several steps are necessary to create a Branded Entertainment deal based on multiple agreements:

- Involve appropriate legal departments early on in the process. Understand that some "evangelism" may be required to ensure legal counsel understands a new way of doing business. This activity usually occurs between the dealmakers and the attorneys.
- As multiple agreements are being created, be sure the timeline for all agreements reflects this complex process. Many times the parties involved tend to focus on the approvals but not on a final executed deal. One of the contracts could potentially trigger financials. A lack of financials due to approvals not already being in place could trigger delays. (The good news is that once the agreements are done, a template will have been created for future deals.)

- Give ample time for the contract process. If you have an estimated schedule, include padding for delays—it will be needed. When lawyers break into new territory, they like to have time to check things thoroughly. Remember that Branded Entertainment deals need to be led by business people not lawyers, but also remember that lawyers are paid to make sure they have covered all the bases for their clients.
- Determine if one person will be allowed to view the agreements between all of the parties. This requirement depends on the sensitivities of the parties involved and the information being disclosed. If no one person is selected, be sure legal counsel clearance from all parties has been given.

Subject areas to watch out for include:

- Accountability
- Ownership of content
- Renewals/sequels
- Results/success measurement/triggers
- Profit motives (Everyone has to be able to make money to feel motivated.)
- Liabilities
- Creativity/leadership
- Financial schedule

Chapter 4 will explore in detail the components of an agreement and provide some options on how to structure contractual relationships.

THE HUMAN COMPONENT

When new ideas or solutions to a problem are suggested, the assumption within many organizations is that new formulas can be applied to particular approaches or existing systems and that, if done correctly, the journey should be successful. After all, success is all about understanding what to do and how to do it. So if all the instructions are spelled out and followed, then why should a solution or new idea not work properly?

People within big organizations are programmed to follow lots of "to-do" maps and to execute as the rules of the game are explained. If told how to do something, then following the to-do maps and the rules should mean that everything will be implemented correctly, but what happens when change comes our way—as it always does.

How does change affect our maps and rules? Following procedures and creating structure are all about the *exterior* side of change. What about the inner world of people inside our organization who have to make change happen?

The thinking processes of each individual inside our organization are actually manifested in their responses to change. When change comes in, survival mechanisms are triggered. This survival response is one of the reasons why new procedures for doing business such as Branded Entertainment do not get automatic buy-in from within an organization. Only when the comfort level has been restored and the change can be seen as an improvement to what exists can a shift can take place.

Now the question becomes how do we approach a new formula or a new way to reinvent media, advertising, and entertainment consumption if the human factor could hinder instead of advance it? This is the real question to answer. Something so intangible should not be that important—but it is. The inner world rules outer manifestations. This dilemma is why it is important to be prepared to look at the big picture of Branded Entertainment, understanding the unspoken roadblocks that may kill a deal before it starts. Let's take a look at a few concepts, elements, and skills that need to be understood and mastered to become a Branded Entertainment expert:

1. Branded Entertainment is not groundbreaking, but it is a departure from how regular business is done between content producers, marketers, and distributors.

2. The initial human resistance factor (the resistance born out of creating change) will automatically be present—guaranteed.

3. The human dynamic needs observation. Observe a group of people on the receiving end of a presentation. See the content idea come to life when presented as a first endeavor on putting people and companies together.

4. A Branded Entertainment deal structure can push people and companies outside of their comfort zones. Add creativity to the table and watch how a collaborative approach expands among the group.

5. Others can start to weigh down what is being shared with their fears and insecurities. This behavior may be in the form of obstacles—real or perceived—lack of research, lack of tangible

results, or concern over "unproven methods"—
all human fear in action.

6. Once the reasons for behavior are obvious, you
   are halfway to the finish line! How so? Well,
   little by little, mastering the art of reading people
   will become a must. By reading people I mean
   understanding what is really inside of them, not
   what they tell you, because what they say is most
   often not what they mean! In situations involving human behavior, knowledge is power. Being
   attentive to the veiled fear and insecurity that
   may potentially derail a deal will give you the
   power to be a better negotiator by coming to the
   table ready to counter fear with facts. Your inner
   "radar" will positively impact the outcome of the
   negotiation—guaranteed.

THE STARTING POINT OF A BRANDED
ENTERTAINMENT DEAL PROPOSITION

Before a deal can take shape, conversations must be held with
the potential participating parties (assuming one person or
company starts the process with an idea that leads to a content idea). I will now share with you a list of some tips and
best practices that have worked during this very initial stage.
The beauty of this list is you can always add to it. This is not
a "how-to" or a "what-to-do" list. It is more like a compilation
of experiences taken from many negotiations that were successful and others that went sour halfway into them.

The primary takeaways from many starts and no-go's
have nothing to do with the ideas shared at the negotiating

table but are more about the group dynamic of those seated around it. My simple strategy:

1. Find a champion whose leadership is obvious to the rest of the group.

2. Take time selecting who that champion will be. Meet with all potential parties to be included and listen. See who could really benefit from championing this process.

3. Simplify the initial briefing about the idea. There will be time later on to better explain the idea.

4. Discuss the business model with a select few. The ones in the group who will only execute will get lost in the big picture of a business proposition.

5. Try to tackle questions in small groups. Avoid a big gathering where several people may gang up and try to kill the process.

6. Start at the top. Have the top person continuously involved until traction is gained from all others, especially those below the leader. People below the leader are sometimes the ones who have the most resistance.

7. Approach the resisters separately. Think of ways whereby they too can gain something personally out of the negotiation.

8. Make the initial approach or conversation personal at first because later you will need connections to close the deal. Connect first and then do business. This approach feels more selective than generic.

9. In business, people like to help friends not strangers. Be a genuine friend first. Take the time necessary to know who is going to be involved on this journey.

10. By the time a conversation is off to possibly becoming a Branded Entertainment deal, some people will have bonded for what could be all of their professional lives. It can be a good bonding or a miserable one. The more you emphasize friendship at first, the better your chances are to have a mutually positive experience.

A reminder. The newness of Branded Entertainment will bring resistance, so the better you are at identifying how to deal with the various parties at the proposition stage, the better off you will be when it is time to focus on the process and execution of a Branded Entertainment deal. Most likely you will need to repeat the pitch process as each party is approached with the idea of doing a potential Branded Entertainment deal together. How to handle the process toward making a deal will be discussed in Chapter 5.

CHAPTER 3

The Players

In the previous two chapters I have provided a breakdown of what Branded Entertainment is as a concept and, conversely, what Branded Entertainment is not. I have also discussed the importance of timing to better understand why making a shift toward Branded Entertainment is optimal now and not later on down the road. Questions that lead to gaining further insight before fully venturing into Branded Entertainment have also been provided. Answers to these questions paved the way to disclosing the components that can make a deal successful.

Now we will move further into understanding who exactly the players are in a Branded Entertainment deal. Some of you may ask: "Isn't it obvious who they are?" If you are a current player in the industry this explanation may indeed be redundant, but for those curious minds who have not yet jumped into the media industry, this is an important time to gain an understanding of who the players are and to decide which side of the negotiating table appeals most to them.

Note: Today's environment is filled with economic turmoil on a worldwide level. Conditions have pushed many to contemplate making a career industry shift. The media industry has a lot to offer. It is an industry that welcomes new ideas and revolutionary thinking. As individuals, we consume media, brands, and entertainment on a daily basis. We live in a society that seeks new ways, new products, and new technology daily. The challenge is to know when and how to evolve. So if you are sitting at a career crossroads, this chapter can help you identify media roles that might suit your future. If you are part of the next generation that has decided to take the time to review the evolution of the media industry, this chapter can be crucial in forming your personal vision of the future in this fast-paced world.

THE MEDIA OUTLETS

Many terms can be used to refer to the vast category of media outlets. Media outlets are the platforms by which groups of people are reached. The number of viewers, consumers, and eyeballs (whatever term you know them by) reached by media outlets varies greatly from one platform to another. The common players are networks, broadcasters, cable, worldwide web (www), and satellite platforms. The ways in which these players reach consumers vary: by air, underground cable, satellite, or digitally. The digital era has brought in a whole new set of "players" that connect to people instantly. The big point of differentiation is that most people no longer connect to media via one primary outlet. Transmission is no longer a one-way exchange. Interactivity is "in" because "interactive" has become the new media.

Throughout this book, I will refer to the media group interchangeably as either media outlets, networks, or media platforms. Any of these terms can be used to refer to the people behind the group leading the decision-making process from within.

The days of the networks being the "gurus" and leading the way to newcomers are fading fast. The entry of new media outlets and platforms has opened up whole new ways to view entertainment, connectivity, and consumers. Networks no longer hold a final say on what goes. Now the consumer has this role. The creation of these new platforms has both amplified their voices by allowing instant feedback from consumers and better quantified their existence by generating significant data about them. The traditional metric of ratings was once without a doubt the game all players had to play—that is no longer the case. The shift is so huge that its consequences are still hard to measure. Not only does the shift change the rules of the game, but it also recalibrates the measure of what success means—all a consequence of the abundance of so many new options fragmenting the market. As a result, for a network, and consequently for a brand, the very definition of what it means to be a success has been forever altered.

Another important evolving fact in media outlets is the direct connection between the media source and the consumer. Now it is possible to communicate individually to each one of them. It is easier to know who consumers are and where they live. Information on what they eat, where they go, and how much money they spend on certain items is also readily available. What a difference from just a decade ago! If you are a newcomer to the media world, the minds of consumers are no longer the enigma they once were for previous generations of professionals. Consumers' minds can now be "deciphered."

This revolution of easy access to consumer information has opened the door for new opportunities. Networks, media companies, and digital platforms are looking for ways to reinvent their business models. Newcomers, you are now quite welcome to step in and ride the wave. This is a time to be remembered in history. It is what I like to refer to as a "bookmark moment." Although the good news is the industry now knows much about consumers, the bad news is the competition is much more ferocious for consumers' attention. Gone are the days when only three or four media options were available to viewers. Today, knowing who the media options are is no longer the issue. Getting customers to stay with a single media outlet as their choice is the current challenge.

Some of you have been in the industry long enough to remember the days when media outlets were run by a group of people who knew how to "get in" and how to "stay in" the inner circle. If you got in early and had experience and the right contacts, you most likely held the power card, but if you were trying to get in and did not have a "godmother" or a "godfather" to open doors for you, your chances were small.

Today the picture is much different. Creativity can get you in the door. Innovation can do wonders. Experience is important but not crucial. If the thinking is forward and it aligns with some out-of-the-box opportunities, then the industry will hear anyone out. Those who sit behind the desks of traditional networks want to hear what is really new and how they can stay in the game. New entrants such as digital platform players, for instance, are excited to be playing along and are scrambling to figure out how to keep viewers the same way the old networks used to (having consumers eating out of the palms of their hands!). A brand's management team still wants to hear how to keep viewers/users captive in the new platforms. The reality is that consumers are no longer captive to a few options. Consumers have become moving targets for the media world in general.

There are many areas within contemporary media outlets where change can be engineered. (*Note*: For the purposes of this book, I will focus on content creation and content delivery. Anything related to engaging, entertaining, and emotionally "catchy" content is regarded as the "golden goose" that everyone wants to own.) Participating as a player on the media outlet side means you hold a very important key inside the media industry. The power on the media side is in knowing who the audience is—even more important is in knowing how to "turn the audience on." Two fundamentals things that those on the media side need to keep in mind to survive are:

- Know why your audience comes to you.
- Know how growth can continue.

The game changer here is figuring out how to best use the information related to the above-mentioned points to drive revenue in a more creative fashion. Content is the answer—as is commonly heard: *build it and they will come.* Hook them with good content and they will stay.

What follows growth? More growth! Better content means attracting a bigger audience. The more the audience grows, the more the platform grows as well. As the platform grows, so will advertisers. This is the business model cycle for content.

This business model cycle is constantly occurring but not necessarily at a desirable growth rate. Brands are attracted once the growth rate turns more attractive, but brands need more than an attractive growth rate to stay. They need to be seduced into something exciting, something inventive—a new way to present what consumers like—that captures more consumers in the process. It is that simple.

Brands are always looking for new ways to present product to the *same* consumers and to *new* consumers. So having new ways to present content that current consumers will like and capturing more consumers are when Branded Entertainment becomes a rational option to be considered by media outlets. Branded Entertainment represents a different way to participate in the business. Branded Entertainment is an inclusive model in which brands can grow in partnership with media outlets (Figure 3.1). Both are invested in a proposition that has some risks, but the partnership can also create some good rewards. Partnership means that both the brands and the media outlets can create something new and both can exploit the potential of content ideas even further through the distribution channels they may already have in existence. For example, a car company can enhance growth through innovative content by expanding the content through the company's dealership channels. The network can also expand a deal by marketing the content through sister channels and within the network's own internet platforms. One goal is common to both: make it grow to be as successful as possible.

One partner alone may not accomplish what is needed. The "bandwidth" achieved by playing solo may not be there to reach "vast and wide" or the timing may be too short to allow reaction by just one player. For instance, a network alone may not gain sufficient instant recognition of a new series unless it taps into a partnership with a brand or a

An Inclusive Model
A Partnership
Brands   Media Outlets

Figure 3.1. The Branded Entertainment model: an inclusive model in which brands and media outlets partner their investments in a proposition with some risk but also with the potential for benefits.

product. The same applies to the other partner: a new product to be launched may not get emotional brand recognition from consumers right away. Consumers may not connect fully to what the product stands for if the brand not associated with the right content. Consumers get "close" to characters; brands therefore need to be close to those characters. The essence can be summed up this way: *A partnership of this nature combines strengths and multiple opportunities, which in return can turn higher profits for both.*

To be a part of an era where networks and consumer platforms are "born overnight" is exciting, but challenges remain. Any newborn network or consumer platform needs to be watched, heard, and followed. If the opportunity is there to create a new way to do business with brands and new emerging platforms, why not take the risk?

THE PRODUCERS

Producers are, for the most part, an independent group, but I am not suggesting that all producers are independent as in not affiliated with a larger, controlling organization. In today's volatile environment, some production companies are being rapidly acquired by networks or are partly owned by agencies. What I am referring to when I speak of independent is more about the independence of producers' thinking processes. I will refer to members of this group interchangeably as producers, production groups, or independent production teams. Any of these terms refer to the people behind the production group leading the decision-making process from within. Producers can be:

- Part of a large production company
- Part of a format creator production company
- A boutique entity with a small group of members
- Freelancers

Producers are always generating ideas. Sometimes producers are the ones who get to produce the idea; sometimes they do not. An idea can sometimes be so big and complex that the producers themselves may not have the capacity to execute the idea. Sometimes a network may only do business with a few trusted production companies that they have worked with over the years. In either case, producers will likely have to work together with other producers.

To better illustrate this point, think of the collaborative work you see every time you watch the credits at the end of a TV show or a movie. Can you recall in recent memory seeing only one company take all the production credit? One company taking all the production credit rarely happens anymore. An exception would be small privately funded productions. These productions operate in much simpler scenarios wherein one company can have the full say on all decisions, including the financial ones. Another exception would be when a production company is big enough to do everything under one roof—then the entire undertaking would be credited to them. With few exceptions, however, most deals include more than a single production company in the mix.

Let's now move to the process of being a producer. As I said earlier, some producers are in the business of generating ideas and making them into a reality. An idea has to be feasible enough to gain traction with others. Otherwise, how much momentum can the idea gain if it cannot be turned into profits or awareness?

One of the best yet simple tools I use is to lay out the idea on paper creatively and financially. Laying out the idea is an important task. Many times, however, I have seen producers avoid this part of the initial process because they do not want to go through endless hours of assembling a treatment and budget unless they have a real "bite" from a client. The mere avoidance of this basic layout work, however, can actually work against the possibility of attaining an approval. If a client, such as a brand or an agency, cannot see the full picture in a one-shot presentation, how can they visualize it and keep moving the ball forward?

The part of an idea being well received and then molded into a presentation is known as "development work."

Producers understand the importance of development work. In this phase, an idea takes shape. The idea is extended into the future to test its viability. This phase is when a big question mark for producers comes up. Does the idea have continuity? If so, the idea may lend itself to longevity within a series. Whether the idea is created as short- or long-form content, the process of evaluating continuity in each piece of the puzzle that turns into an episode is a must. During this phase it is important to make ideas "bulletproof." To be bulletproof, ideas have to pass trial tests. Assign several people to the development work—people who are qualified to answer questions such as:

- Is there a real audience for the idea?
- Does the idea fill a gap that no one else is serving?
- Is the idea engaging enough to maintain momentum?
- Will there be potential growth once the idea is out in the media world?

As simple as these questions may sound, they tend to put ideas through the ultimate test. The answers to other questions about the idea (the budget and production) have to be clear and compelling and have strong research backing when needed (Figure 3.2). Producers can save a lot of time and effort by following these simple steps and folding the answers to these questions into the initial presentation.

The next part of the production process is planning the budget. Once the "natural high" born out of creativity in the development process has worn off, it is time to come back to reality and assemble a budget. Planning the budget is another important step because having a role in production implies

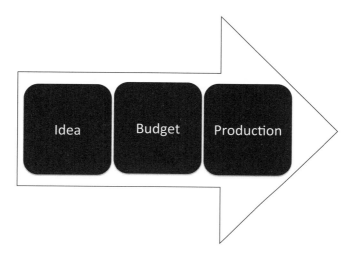

Figure 3.2. Bulletproofing an idea: obtain qualified answers to questions about the idea, the budget, and production from developmental work and research; then incorporate the answers in an initial presentation.

there has to be an understanding of the financials involved. The budget process has several elements (Figure 3.3), with much to consider along the way:

- Assemble an initial budget: This process, known as the *first pass*, is created for all parties to understand the overall picture and the cost of what is required to put the idea in motion. The first pass does not need to have exact figures. Some figures will only be estimates until more information is available about how the idea is going to be carried out.

- Review the first pass: Go over the figures with the parties potentially involved in the deal and be prepared to act on revisions. New variables can be brought to the table at this time about certain specifics of the production.

- Establish a working budget: Once revisions have been made, it is time to establish a *working budget*. The working budget is not considered a final budget until all parties have signed off on it. The purpose of a working budget is to have a structure in place that is viewed favorably by all parties so you can get the ball rolling and start preproduction planning.

- Finalize the budget: As preproduction planning begins to draw in real-world data and ongoing negotiations start to wind down, it is now time to reach conclusions toward a *final budget* in conjunction with the final contract (at least, attempt to reach conclusions at this point as shown in Figure 3.3). This working document should be part of the contract appendix.

Next in the process are the three steps of production: preproduction, production, and postproduction. (*Note*: For matters of correlation with the title of this book, it's important to mention that Branded Entertainment is largely intertwined in each one of these steps.)

Preproduction. In this phase, a producer has no choice but to be a multi-tasker. The producer will most likely assemble a small team to orchestrate the details necessary to properly carry out the production of the idea. This group is called the preproduction team. Each preproduction period has a unique set of goals that are usually determined during the budget process. It is common to see the budget assembly

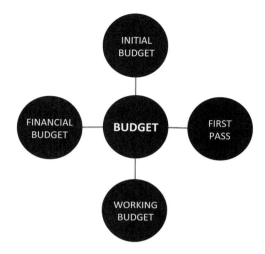

Figure 3.3. Elements of the budgeting process.

process occur during preproduction time. Preproduction is also when the rest of the team starts to come on board for the production. All necessary paperwork is handled and reviewed during this phase

Production. Production is when all thinking and planning move into action. The schedule and the time necessary to carry out the full production—known as the *timeline*—are the responsibility of the producer in charge of production and the production management team. Producers actively discuss shoot details with the other members of the deal: the agency and the brand leaders. Bear in mind that each production may differ in style and process. (The production process is beyond the scope of this book. The steps in this section are therefore basic. Numerous online sources can provide additional information.)

Postproduction. Postproduction is an area many people in the business think of as the easiest part—but it is not. Postproduction can be quite tricky, actually. The content has been shot, but not until it is time to sit in the edit suites can a determination be made as to how well the production goals have been accomplished. This caution is why I strongly advise, if possible, to bring content editors to the actual shoot. The headaches that can be resolved by adding post-crew to the budget end up, many times, saving production some hard core dollars. During postproduction, creativity comes alive. The combination of the shoot itself plus artistic flavor from the director in selecting all other elements makes postproduction a unique experience. Postproduction is the time when graphics, music, and effects come into play. It is also when the work is reviewed and finally approved by the other parties. This time is a fascinating side of the business.

THE AGENCIES

Agencies today have grown and multiplied in the Branded Entertainment industry. Big agencies have branched out, and specialty shops have sprouted. Meanwhile, smaller agencies have become very focused on particular skills and have narrowed down their menus of offerings to clients. Agencies have now grown more and more comfortable with fragmenting the pieces of the business to multiple agencies, depending on the strength of each shop. (For the purposes of this book, agencies are also referred to as shops, groups, or services.) Going back to basics, advertising agencies are considered middlemen in Branded Entertainment transactions. Brands are the clients of agencies. One purpose of agencies is to look after a brand's business, short and long term.

Today's agency business model. The original blueprint of the ad agency business, back when the model was simple, encompassed looking after the media, creative content, public relations, promotions, and the marketing needs for a brand. Later, other pieces were added to the core business of agencies such as digital, direct marketing, etc. Then, over the years, small vertical groups started to handle bigger pieces of the business, big enough pieces to cause them to consider branching out into smaller (or not so small these days) agencies or groups that would focus only on a certain area of expertise. So in addition to traditional ad agencies, we now have:

- *Specialty creative shops* focusing on the creative work for the brand mainly related to the message to the target consumer
- *Media buying services* specializing in the negotiation of ad time with a goal to get the most amount of ad time from the media outlets for the least amount of money
- *Digital agencies* centering on creation, actualization, and revamping of digital media residing primarily in cyberspace

This structure of agencies, shops, and services is relevant to our subject matter of Branded Entertainment because finding the gatekeeper within an agency is key to igniting the possibility of a Branded Entertainment deal. Branded Entertainment is considered a business creative transaction, meaning business and creative leaders within an agency are

Figure 3.4. Inside an agency: the key components to an evolved Branded Entertainment strategy.

the targets of the approach. Nowadays, a client branches out business for one brand to different agencies, depending on a particular need, making knowing where to start conversations for branded content complex, confusing, and difficult. Brand leaders from the client side sometimes do not even know which agency should lead the way on a new business transaction of this nature. To be "inside" the agency world is to be part of an enormous traffic control system where multiple businesses are interacting with one another and multiple layers of the brand's business are being developed one right after another. Add to this complexity the fact that the overall business is rapidly changing and evolving according to new market needs (Figure 3.4).

A new reality. Agencies typically pride themselves on being the creative source for ideas, systems, and optimization tools. They want to be an efficient foundation for a brand's business. An agency's image is closely linked to their creative work. When successfully executed, an agency's work can further evolve the personality of a brand. Being recognized as the architect of that type of evolution is like hitting the jackpot in the industry. A true win can attract new business like bees are drawn to nectar. The wins and losses in the agency business are publicly known; hence, everyone keeps a scorecard. Agencies keep a close eye on each other's business knowing that any creative hit that wins awards and media recognition can launch an agency or the competitors to the top of the game. The business that agencies conducted for their brands years ago has been permanently altered. We now have the trickling effect of breakups, mergers, and segmentation. Smaller shops are much more capable of handling a leaner and more effective infrastructure. Some hire young and inexperienced talent. By opening the gate to these newcomers, agencies hope to get in return high creativity levels from untainted individuals who have not picked up bad habits from other agencies. Similar to the media outlets, the agency business has grown and fragmented to such degree that it is not enough to just be part of the mix—it is all about joining forces and offering unique possibilities to clients.

A new revenue model. The next reality in the life of an agency is the ever-changing revenue model. Agencies traditionally were paid a fee or a percentage based on the amount of business managed. Fees and percentages were in the 10 and even 15% range. Well, those days are history. The entire compensation system has drastically been lowered, so much so that agencies have had to learn to cut new deals for themselves. Undercutting one another in order to win business is commonly seen in agency battles for a new account. A problem that often arises with this method is the agency may end up winning the business, but that is no guarantee that the percentage fee or flat fee negotiated will be good enough or fair enough to keep the business growing.

Despite the stark realities that face many agencies, excitement still remains on this side of the business. When the battle is on for a particular brand's business, agencies compete head to head against each other. An agency team must work together to succeed. The competition is ferocious. The rush of being in the game is exhilarating, but just as excitement peaks when chasing a deal, it quickly fades once the assignment is landed and the clock starts ticking on providing value for the client.

Pitching Branded Entertainment to Agencies

Mindset is everything when nurturing newly acquired business. Once a deal is assigned and secured, the agency team hired to handle the postacquisition phase will run at a different pace. The mindset of the team changes as it goes from rush, rush, rush to maintenance mode. The maintenance mode is more like: *keep it, don't lose it, or don't fix it if it ain't broken.* The mid-level employees who maintain the brands are also the ones who decide if a new piece of business is worth reviewing. Their collective mindset of not altering something that is working with something new can make entry rather difficult. Yet only by being allowed "in" does the possibility of a branded deal coming together even start. My suggestion is to find out who is working to maintain the brands you are targeting and be aware when approaching them that their natural instincts may be to act as a gatekeeper against allowing anything new. Also find out who the leaders are above this level and attempt to spark a first meeting with one of them. Leaders at the next level have experience in managing new ways to cut a deal—which can be exciting for those in leadership roles.

Some homework items to research and think through before attempting to initiate a potential Branded Entertainment deal include:

- Know the leaders: Find out who the internal senior players in the agency are because they hold a big role in new deals, especially branded content. These individuals have the power to keep the level of interest in an idea high while it is being assessed and evaluated.

- Clarify agency compensation: Have a plan about how to compensate the agency and be clear about it. If the agency world is already ultracompetitive and saturated, how else can the agency be approached from the start if not with incremental revenue?

- Know the brand: When I say "know the brand" I mean know *everything* about it. I cannot tell you how many times I have been told by agencies that the one thing that turns them off almost immediately is when they are in a meeting and being pitched an idea for content and the presenter has no clue as to how the brand can properly fit into the content idea.

- Make the mix "right:" An initial approach to an agency should carry the right amount of creative on the idea being presented and the right amount of business points to define what success will mean. Having balance between these two areas can generate a fair amount of interest, certainly enough to keep the process rolling.

It is not enough to be good at generating ideas. Also crucial is knowing how ideas can be monetized for the brand *and* for the agency. Agencies are in this deal to make money. Forgetting this notion is a common newcomer's mistake. A first-time branded content deal can be shuttered by an inexperienced assumption by the proposing party that the agency knows how the compensation will work for them from the new endeavor. How agency compensation will work is a business point that needs to be spelled out just like the idea itself. Why so? The amount of work this new piece of business will mean to the existing staff is not minimal; the compensation should not be either.

Truth be told, other players can forget that agencies need incremental revenue. The base agreement between the agency and the brand sometimes is not enough to keep the agency business profitable, especially when engaged in Branded Entertainment deals. So the idea of generating new business with incremental fees for the agency can be attractive if positioned properly. After all, Branded Entertainment is not a "business as usual" proposition—the model of doing business as partners should include fair compensation for all.

Agency Roles

As shown in Figure 3.5, an agency can participate in a new Branded Entertainment business model in several ways:

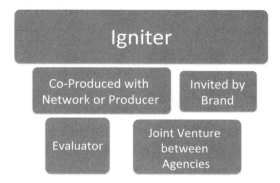

Figure 3.5. Agency participation in the new Branded Entertainment business model.

1. An agency can ignite the idea for a Branded Entertainment deal, run it by the client, and then approach multiple networks with producers to make it happen.

2. An agency can be approached by a network or by a producer with an idea and, in turn, the agency can take the idea to their client. Basically, the agency would brief all corresponding brand leaders that would be involved in approving the decision. At some point in this process, the agency could invite the creators of the idea to help out in pitching it to all internal levels of the brand required to make a final decision.

3. An agency can be asked to participate in a new deal by an existing client. The client may have a need or may have been approached directly by a network or producers. The idea has gained traction internally at the brand level so the client has

decided it is time to invite their own agency to
analyze the idea and make recommendations.

4. A client retaining more than one agency can
    decide to engage a creative shop in the initial pro-
    cess. By the time the idea takes shapes, a media/
    marketing agency is invited in with the purpose
    of reviewing the proposition, evaluating finan-
    cials, and recommending media extensions.

5. One agency may be working jointly with an out-
    side party such as a network or producer on a
    particular branded idea. To unify a proposition
    and take it jointly to the brand, the agency may
    need the other client's agency backing.

If the agency holds true to its purpose, the agency should
manifest this purpose in a Branded Entertainment startup by
having several of the agency's constituencies participate during different stages of the deal. These stages include, but are
not limited to, creativity, negotiations, marketing, account
management, promotions, public relations, and digital. Large
agencies and boutique shops are good candidates to participate in Branded Entertainment deals—the selection varies
greatly depending on the skills and expertise that can be
brought to the table. This is an exciting side of the business
to be on in the vast space of the media world.

New branded content business run through an agency
can be accomplished via multiple pathways. Throughout my
career in branded content, I have been involved in each of
these scenarios, which is why I keep mentioning that each
deal and the time it takes to complete the deal are unique.
Naturally, as the number of players involved increases, the
time required to bring a deal to fruition will increase. As

a base rule, anytime you are dealing with more than one agency, the plot will thicken, but understanding all the different ways in which an agency can participate in the process is a good step toward simplifying the timing for a deal to be completed.

THE BRANDS

In this book, the terms brand(s), advertiser, or client are used interchangeably to refer to the companies/products/ services which, as a primarily goal, exist to serve a need for consumers (viewers). A brand serves a purpose in the consumer marketplace. Consumers come to know brands either by personal consumption experiences or through the media, which creates awareness for a particular target customer. We are most familiar with the concept of creation of awareness and know it as *traditional advertising*. Traditional advertising involves the creation of ad campaigns that can take on many forms. Ads can be experienced in seconds—10, 15, 30, or 60—and even in minutes (infomercials), depending on the goal and the media outlet being used.

Brand managers are the custodians of a brand. Brand managers nurture an entire marketing process that includes, but is not limited to, product development, marketing, budgetary parameters, and distribution strategies. The parent company of a brand can be an umbrella for many other brands. Some of these brands are related to the same category and some are not. In the advertising world, brands are also known as *advertisers*. Brands become the clients of agencies and media outlets and are ranked in the advertising world according to the total amount of their media spend. Brands that belong to large conglomerates usually rank very high in terms of importance. These brands also derive benefit from being part of a parent company with many brands under the same umbrella. This ranking has an impact when sitting at a table to negotiate with the media world. Leverage is key because volume usually dictates the terms and the agency or media outlet that has the best offering for the brand.

Brands have had a protagonist role in the history of Branded Entertainment. For instance, in the early days of television, a brand's participation meant being "inside" a show, not "around" it. Brand participation was how the networks financed expensive productions. In return, the brand logo, jingle, and message would be inside the content. The audience would sing along to those jingles and the host would recite the brand's message right in the middle of the script of a particular TV show. In fact, nationwide audiences became so used to the idea that a brand was part of the show that later on show recall was as important as the brand itself. TV viewers came to know a jingle so well that they could recall it for others. They knew about the brand being advertised as much as they knew about the show itself. An example is the song *See the U.S.A. In Your Chevrolet*, better known as being a commercial jingle from circa 1949. Written for the Chevrolet Division of General Motors Corporation, the song was sung by Peter Lind Hayes and Mary Healy, a husband and wife duo, and was the Chevrolet jingle heard during the show *Inside U.S.A. with Chevrolet*. This association of Chevrolet with the song was already an authentic, ideal precedent before the song became associated with Dinah Shore through Chevrolet's decade-long sponsorship of her television shows. Later on, the song became one of Shore's signature songs. In the Branded Entertainment world, this type of

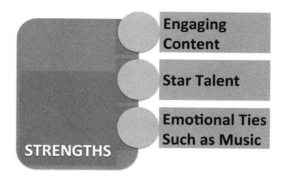

Figure 3.6. Strengths of an ideal Branded Entertainment scenario: content, talent, and an emotional bond with consumers.

association is called an "ideal scenario." The example of the Chevrolet jingle has three strengths (Figure 3.6):

- Long-lasting, engaging content
- A good association with star talent
- A musical element with an emotional tie to consumers

The next wave (or generation) in advertising was quite a departure from the good old days when "brands = an emotional connection"—days that have become a distant memory. "Appointment viewing" had started to fade. This new wave or evolution in advertising brought with it a revolution in technology that focused more on content *only* when viewers needed or wanted it. This type of content focus is now known as *on demand*. On-demand content focus redirected the destiny of brands and media. Accounts of the history of this evolving relationship between brands and media show that their relationship has come full circle:

from once being so united that a brand almost could not be separated from content, to being all about content with the presence of the brand being almost disruptive, to now being reunited again—content and brand together on multiple screens. Branded Entertainment brings back the time when brand and content were like one. In this environment, brands need a "hand" to guide them to new ways to reconnect with consumers. Brands also need to understand how this new business formula will work for them. Brands want to belong to a functional partnership where the old days feel like new again. A Branded Entertainment strategy must first ignite a brand manager's curiosity. Then when then idea is shared with the parties potentially involved in the deal, the possibilities can be imagined and the willingness to try something new increases.

THE PLAYERS MEET

Having a basic understanding of who the players are helps to create a better understanding of how these players will interact with each other during a potential Branded Entertainment deal. Now that the basic function of each player is known, it is time to disclose how these players will meet. How the players meet does not imply that the only way a branded deal can happen is if the players all meet at once. The sequence of meetings can be different from deal to deal. The key thing is to understand that all parties will participate from the start.

Participation of all parties from the start is one of the biggest differences between a Branded Entertainment deal and a "sponsorship" media deal. In a sponsorship deal, one or two parties can agree to create something of value and later decide to take the idea to a third party who might buy into it. In this arrangement, the creativity factor still resides primarily in the hands of the originators. The needs taken into consideration for the content created also usually come from the parties who started the process. When new players (sponsors) join halfway into this type of arrangement, the needs of the new players might be "forced" into the content rather than being included organically or naturally.

In Branded Entertainment, the needs of all parties are put on the table from the start. The possibilities that arise are far greater when all parties create together. The starting point is fueled with power from all the parties being engaged as a new sense of collective ownership is born, ultimately making Branded Entertainment deals more fruitful and rewarding.

The tactical ways in which all parties meet can vary. For instance, a producer may already have a relationship with an agency so the first meeting occurs between the producer and the agency. (This scenario assumes that the agency is up to speed with the current needs of their client, a brand.) Immediately afterward, the next meeting is with a media outlet. The ultimate goal is to meet with a brand. At this meeting, all possibilities are presented to the brand in an effort to demonstrate that a brand-centric process is in the works with a Branded Entertainment idea. An ideal scenario is when the brand is invited to the table. The agency and content producers are asked to participate side by side with a media outlet to fulfill the brand's objectives.

No matter how a Branded Entertainment idea starts, the brand must be in mind from the beginning. With this understanding established, let's discuss three strategies I recommend at this very early stage. I call these strategies the "Three I's:" Immerse, Identify, and Initiate (Figure 3.7):

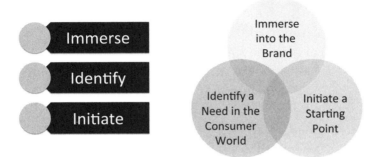

Figure 3.7. The three I's. Early-stage strategies for a Branded Entertainment idea: immerse, identify, and initiate.

- *Immerse* into the possibilities—with an in-depth understanding of a brand and its attributes.
- *Identify* a need—an unfulfilled space in the content world.
- *Initiate* a starting point—a seed from which all starts and grows.

Immerse into the Possibilities

Not until we are willing to become "brand obsessive" can we see the possibilities and what could emerge from them. A brand is more than a name. A brand is more than a style or status. Brands have a life and a personality. Media people tend to forget that. An in-depth understanding of the brand means to become intimate with the personality of that brand. So what does "intimate" mean in this context? Becoming intimate with the personality of a brand means knowing several things about the brand. If there were no "label" for a particular brand, what attributes would perfectly match the personality of the brand? Which characters would personify the brand? What do these characters stand for? What emotions are evoked? Aside from the brand's regular basic use, what are extended uses or applications that the brand/product can have? What are the nontraditional uses? What are the not-so-well-known uses for a potential new consumer? Can the brand's reach be extended to a nontraditional target audience?

Brand managers, consumer research, and a brand's ad agency possess the "know-how" and the "right information" to understand the brand from an intimate perspective. In this case, an overview of a brand from 30,000 feet above just will not do. We must turn into scholars of the brand when sitting at the deal table, especially if any of us think we already know everything there is to know about a brand.

Consumers can teach us a lot. Social media has become the voice of end users. Consumers and social media can show us the "blind spots" of a brand and additional uses of the same brand/product, aspects which sometimes are innocently ignored by experts on the brand. Teaming up with the resources of new media and engaging in a "think tank" listening experience with consumers are great ways to embark on a mission of discovering new possibilities.

Once we truly understand the brand, we need to ask this question: "Where are areas in which the brand is not fulfilling its mission?" Follow this question with:

- Is the brand not reaching its total target audience?
- Has the brand saturated its position by name, yet not delivered enough on usage, innovative applications, or digital extensions?

- Is market share declining while other competitors are gaining momentum?
- Does the brand know and understand "a real intimacy" with its consumers?

These questions will trigger interesting answers. The answers are clues for moving toward a branded content deal. In today's media environment, no brand is consistently 100% sure about the right formula to connect with consumers—if the brand is sure, the lifetime of the content is short. The explosion of options is so vast and continuous that sometimes brands even question their own approaches to growth. By doing so, they are constantly seeking and searching out what other brands are doing, possibly better or differently, which is why the approach to growth needs to be diagnostic in nature:

- Listen, listen, listen to other brands. (You just might learn something new!)
- As questions such as those above are answered, look for the void they themselves are not finding internally.
- Ask questions that suggest a venture into the "new." (Has your brand reached its full potential across its wide marketing reach? Can your brand expand to a different target group?)

These are tough questions to answer. The answers do not lie on the surface. Some "digging" needs to happen for the real answers to appear. *Remember*: Branded Entertainment solutions are not for all brands, but for the brands that can answer "yes," a Branded Entertainment solution will work—a branded deal for the brand will be like a custom-made glove is to a hand.

Identify a Need

Once a content idea has been developed, approach media outlets with the idea. The content idea should fit a particular need the network or the media outlet has—whether they already know it or not. This contact is considered to be an initial meeting. The identity of the brand is *not* disclosed at this time. The purpose of the initial meeting is to present only the content idea itself and to identify a gap in the network's programming grid. Important to mention here is that that this branded team should have researched the network's audience and its patterns well ahead of time. Researching the network's audience and patterns helps identify gaps that exist in the network's current approach (by "gap," I mean an unfulfilled need for an audience). If a gap is acknowledged by the network, it can be the start of a good deal.

By wearing the hat of content creators, the branded team's goal is to reach an understanding with the network that sparks new creativity. Even if ideas have to be modified later on, the important thing is that there is acceptance from the beginning to execute and to create content.

Once the team has initial acceptance from the network, more information needs to be gathered regarding related content and the other media competitors. Again, remember to listen, listen, listen. The purpose of this meeting is to receive information, not to recite a monologue!

Words of caution: Remain flexible with variables such as talent/host/participants. Your team may have the perfect fit for these variables, but so may the network or media outlet. This is a time when a high level of compromise is needed from all other parties involved. Also be very savvy when proposing potential time periods for the new content. If the content is to be live on the Internet, the time period is not as big an issue, but if the time period involves cable or broadcast content be sure to have done your homework before making any suggestions about the time period.

Important: Again, I emphasize that the brand is *not* to be fully disclosed at a first meeting because the goal of the meeting is to address various priorities. The top priority at this early stage is to present the content idea itself and to identify a missing gap inside the network's programming grid. Not disclosing the brand is a strategic call. The course of action inside the network after an idea has been presented is that the idea goes through different departments for approval where the internal network supporters will champion the idea to others (e.g., to follow protocol).

Make the Pitch

The pitch occurs at a separate meeting. The brand is included in this meeting, making this meeting different from the initial meeting when no attachment of the brand to the content idea was made. Basic elements of the pitch include:

- A simple idea—simple to understand, simple to explain
- A question at the beginning to trigger the curiosity of the audience
- Use of "what if …" to present different scenarios and help clarify the idea in the minds of the audience
- Use of few words on visual presentations—stand-alone sentences centered on a single page are best
- Use of images to create vivid mental connections

- Disclosure of the full idea by making an association that is recognizable by the audience ("The
  Amazing Race meets the NFL" is an example of
  this type of association. Most people have watched
  The Amazing Race or at least have heard about it.
  Who has not heard of the NFL? These two entities convey a particular message. When linked
  together they can provide a visual connection for
  the type of association you are trying to achieve.)

The pitch will be discussed in more detail in Chapter 4.

Some say "the devil is in the details." I always say "heaven
is in the planning." Either way, *plan everything in advance*.
Be very aware of the titles of the people attending meetings.
Using the example of an idea and a network discussed earlier in this chapter, first in the rounds of network meetings
will be meeting with mostly programming or development
people. Second will be meetings when the brand becomes
engaged once the idea is within the network or the media
outlet. At this stage, participation of ad sales and production
may come into the mix. Until all the parties that make a deal
occur have met (a minimum being the brand, the network,
and the producers), the content idea is only a "big bang"
theory!

Initiate a Starting Point

Once a diagnostic approach has led to identifying where a
void may be inside a media outlet and debriefing about the
brand has taken place, it is time to develop the seed that will
sprout a new beginning for the brand. Out of this seed, a
multitude of ideas can be developed. The ideas can come in

the form of a TV show, a movie, a promotional tool, webisodes, or even a theme for a new advertising campaign. The ideas can then be explored one by one until the right one can be attached to the brand.

The seed is born from a team who now understands the brand from all angles. This team is not composed of brand people, but of content creators who understand viewers as an audience with a vast appetite for content, which changes rapidly according to trends and fads. This core group understands that good content matched with an appropriate look and feel and the right tonality can break the waves of monotony within the vast world of media options.

CHAPTER 4

Starting
the Process

With an understanding of the concepts in play and an introduction to the key players, we can now turn our attention to the process itself. To begin, we must first familiarize ourselves with the three primary components necessary to successfully bring forward a Branded Entertainment initiative: the idea, the team, and the agreements. Once these must-haves are in place, we will look at the early output necessary from both the drivers of the process and the nascent team to get a deal off the ground (Figure 4.1).

THE IDEA

Ideas—and being able to work with them—are main reasons why so many people love the Branded Entertainment business. Doesn't it seem obvious why? Talk to people. Everyone has an idea for a show, a series, or a particular character. Some ideas are good, some are average, but the point is ideas

Figure 4.1. The three primary components and the early output necessary to start the Branded Entertainment process.

run through our heads constantly. People who make a living from the development of ideas often say coming up with ideas is like using a muscle that becomes strengthened over time—the more you use it, the easier it gets. For these people, tapping this source is like exercising a muscle. (Apparently they exercise their brain muscles more often than the rest of us!)

I have always been curious about understanding where ideas come from. From my days of devouring Jungian psychology books, I adopted one simple understanding about ideas and their source. Ideas come from a source called *consciousness*. Within the vast space of consciousness, one type of consciousness in particular catches my attention: *collective* consciousness. As I have come to interpret it, collective consciousness—the common ether space we share as humans—is where inspiration, wisdom, and creativity are born. The collective consciousness is a space we humans have and can access. This space is where the business of creation begins. Have you heard someone say they have a great idea but do not really know where it came from? Ideas stem from the collective source of inspiration, better known as the collective consciousness. What resonates most to me is that anyone can access collective consciousness. All of us can tap into this amazing source to some degree. Some creative gurus in the media and entertainment business are very familiar with the collective consciousness and have mastered use of it to get their "juices" flowing. All of us have the potential to be creators of great ideas, which is a main reason why group gatherings to brainstorm are more common than ever.

Brainstorming is now part of most creative processes. Brainstorming groups should be made up of people from different constituencies and age groups. The sessions can be informal. One never knows who will be the one to tap into their collective consciousness source and bring forth the next brilliant idea! I recommend conducting brainstorming sessions under a simple rule: If an idea is about to be discarded, the only reason is that someone in the group has suggested something better to replace it. Brainstorming sessions are opportunities in which an idea can be developed and later taken to other groups to be further explored. Secondary groups of people who give their opinions and thoughts on how to improve an idea can also help find an outlet for the idea. Important to remember is that unbiased opinions can bring bits of information that may contribute to further refining an idea.

Creating brainstorming sessions around an idea is not new, but in Branded Entertainment making each session very goal centric is necessary. For example, one goal can be to test all the social media opportunities the idea can generate. Another goal can be to select the best type of ideas based on the group's consensus. Once the idea is clear, next is making it "bulletproof" for the audience that will hear the pitch.

Being *bulletproof* means that several key questions have been precisely answered (Figure 4.2):

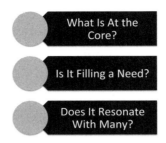

Figure 4.2. Key questions to answer about a content idea.

- What is at the core of this idea?
- Does this idea fill a need that is not being met?
- Does this idea resonate with many people? How? Explain.

Next are questions concerning looking into the future and getting comfortable with the vision of the idea:

- Does the idea have "legs" to keep it growing/moving forward?
- Does the idea have clear potential for all parties involved?
- Can the idea live on multiple platforms?
- Is the idea based on a story or a theme that has the opportunity to evolve over time or is it a one-time-only deal?
- Can the idea be monetized?

All of these questions must be answered before moving on toward creating a pitch. These questions can be directed to a group that is representative of opinions that mimic an audience's reaction. Having clarity concerning the answers to these questions minimizes the risks associated with failing to make an outstanding first impression on a potential new party. (Remember from Chapter 3 that minimizing risk is a huge part of the content production process. Minimizing risk is the art that differentiates average dealmakers from great dealmakers.)

The final step in the idea development process is to turn the idea into a pitch. This is a "not-to-be-missed" step that is done prior to writing a *treatment*, which is when the idea shapes up and outlines the arc of the idea and its "tonality" (the feelings, perceptions, etc. to be communicated by the idea). Then a short or long treatment will need development. (Developing and writing the pitch will be discussed later in this chapter.)

Ideas are accessible to everyone. Ideas are "hooks." They are seductive. They seduce us when we have them and they seduce us when we hear them. The manifestation of ideas is the fuel that makes the business of content creation fun. As the process starts for Branded Entertainment opportunities, the search for ideas comes to life. Deciding which ones are worth exploring is an important step. Realization that not all of the ideas are suitable for development comes next from the refinement process. The reasons to choose one idea versus another vary greatly. The goal—what dealmakers need to care about—is to understand the nature of an idea and what it can bring to the table for a brand. Having the right idea is one of the pillars of a Branded Entertainment deal but not the entire foundation (more on this later). Thoroughly evaluate the nature of the content idea and its potential to be a solid pillar.

The content idea will be covered at an initial meeting that has the purpose of seeing if there can be an engagement from a party such as a network or media outlet. The content idea must be good enough for media outlets to want it. The brand must be well placed to fill a void or to address a current consumer need. Next is determining who should be part of the ideal team to make a Branded Entertainment deal come to life.

THE TEAM

The ideal Branded Entertainment team must undertake several important considerations with no vested interest in favoring any of the participating sides: the media outlets, the brand/agency, or the independent producers. The team's mission is to serve the overall deal, not the individual goals of the participating parties. "Must haves" for the team are people from each of the participating groups—together these people will enable the parts of a potential deal to come together. The initial team can have members added or replaced as details advance and more parties decide to confirm their participation.

For example, an initial branded team can be comprised of an agency leader who is searching for the right idea to propose to a client/brand. The second member can be the creator of a content idea with potential to become a branded content idea. This second member understands how to build extensions to this idea, carries the negotiation forward, and keeps the process moving with possible media outlets. As the conversation turns into a "maybe" with a media partner, a new member would join this team: a person designated by the network/outlet. The branded team is now comprised

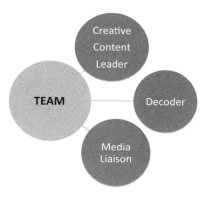

Figure 4.3. Suggested roles of branded team members.

of three members who together will strategize and develop the proposal that would then be taken to the brand for final approval.

Team member options vary depending on who leads the deal from the start. Regardless of who ignites the deal, however, I believe certain skills are extremely important to have in the mix of the right team. I have given the team members names to approximate their roles: creative content leader, decoder, and media liaison (Figure 4.3):

- Creative content leader skills:
  - Has already thought out the idea very well
  - Understands the idea evolution process inside a team setting
  - Initially is not concerned with brand integration possibilities until the idea has been fleshed out; once the idea is developed is comfortable creating seamless brand integrations

- Decoder skills:
  - Has a well-rounded understanding of the brand's purpose and knows what can or cannot be done with the brand
  - Understands the process of locating the brand's touch points and emotionally connecting with consumers
  - Has access to the history of the brand with sup-ported research that can point out what has worked well in the past and what has not
- Media liaison skills:
  - Ensures viability and support for the success of the entire deal with promotional campaigns, media buys, and 360-degree extensions
  - Has participated in creating short- and long-form content; does not assume that creating short content is the same as the long-content experience
  - Can connect with other departments from the different parties participating in the Branded Entertainment initiative (Each party has goals to meet after the branded deal is done. Crossing boundaries and communicating effectively to alert all parties of opportunities that may come from this deal are skills required of the media liaison.)

THE RIGHT AGREEMENT

The right agreement is not only a very important part of the Branded Entertainment process, but it is also the reason why many people shy away from doing these unique transactions. As exciting as the creative process can be, liability and accountability questions will immediately arise. At times, liability and accountability questions can overshadow the higher good in the overall deal.

Over the course of many branded agreements and many prospect explorations, one thing never changes—the quick and simple question asked by the skeptics: "Can you show me an example of an agreement?" Providing a sample agreement may seem like an easy thing to do, but it is not. I do not know where examples of branded agreements are available (except for this book). Even now when almost anything can be found on the web, including templates for all kinds of business and agreement contracts, I have yet to find anything for Branded Entertainment agreements.

My early experiences showed that over time Branded Entertainment deals were making "history." As each new agreement was reached, I also noticed that no two deals were exactly alike. So in this vast area of possibilities and opportunities, I finally realized we in the Branded Entertainment business also had to be the creators of the business transaction. Having a great idea and taking it to partners or just having a team create an idea was not enough. Pivotal was knowing how to craft the idea on paper with all the appropriate responsibilities and liabilities outlined.

My experiences led me to go directly to media attorneys who understood the business of content, negotiations with networks, and sponsorships deals. These media attorneys, however, also did not have quick references for how to assemble a Branded Entertainment agreement. Navigating through something this new was a mystery to them as well. (I called it "the road less traveled.") After going back and forth with several attorneys, my realization was simple: the best choice was to sit down with an attorney and explain the mechanics of how a deal was coming together. During multiple client/attorney sessions, the goals of each party had to be disclosed, along with the reasons for coming to the table. Finance models also had to be developed to get the deal off the ground. The rest of the details still needed some figuring out. They would form part of the negotiations that would follow—things such as:

- How much money is considered to be profit?
- What will a future deal look like if all goes well?
- Who will handle a "tie break" if there is disagreement on the creative or business side?

With some basic information in hand, an agreement could then start to come to life and become the skeleton of the branded deal. This skeleton would need reviewing by the parties so they could add or delete sections that were not fully covering or protecting them. The skeleton was a first draft, not meant to serve as the entire deal. The skeleton did not require all parties to participate. Certain terms, however, were important to all and these needed to be reviewed. The purpose of the skeleton was to ensure that all the "basics" were there. Due to confidentiality concerns, however, all the basics might not be able to be included in one agreement.

The challenging part of this process is to get attorneys from all sides to look at something new in an ordinary amount of time. Many attorneys new to Branded Entertainment deals fear they could miss something because they do not have first-hand experience in how deals like this play out. Most in-house attorneys from the networks and agencies are quite used to working with existing templates from which they quickly gather the knowledge of what is required to protect their companies and minimize risk. In the case of Branded Entertainment deals, however, attorneys have to look for things they have not yet even explored. (*Note*: One way to tackle a new contract template is to conduct an exercise of creating hypothetical scenarios of what could happen "if this or that." This process, however, can be a rigorous exercise requiring the dealmakers at the table to be sitting side-by-side with the attorneys. Be aware of the obvious: time can fly which means so can attorney fees.)

One pressing question everyone is interested in having an answer for is: "How many agreements should there be?" In a perfect world, having everything fit under one agreement would be nice. Believe me, I spent many hours and many sleepless nights during my first deals thinking about the possibility of having everything under one template. I asked for the same from the attorneys. The intention to have a single template was always there, but reality turned out differently. The reason was simple: no single party has full and total control over the entire agreement.

Having a one-template scenario, like a buyer/seller agreement in real estate, is nice in theory but hard to execute in real time in Branded Entertainment negotiations. Multiple parties are involved—anywhere from three (network, brand, producer) to sometimes four (network, brand, agency, producer) to even more than five if multiple brands participate (Figure 4.4). This statement does not mean there cannot be one agreement at some point, but a "one-agreement" scenario requires a willingness from all parties to allow disclosure of intimate details while building an overall agreement. To date, I have not seen that willingness happen.

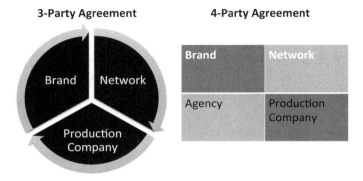

Figure 4.4. Participating parties in three- and four-party agreements.

Asking all parties involved to disclose all details to everyone is difficult. A network may already have a deal in place with an agency. The agency may request that the network make this deal part of their overall larger deal, but the details of the agreement may pertain only to the agency and not involve any other party in the Branded Entertainment agreement. These details should therefore remain private and not be disclosed to others.

Another example can help convey the nature of privacy in the process. An advertising agency could be leading the Branded Entertainment team. The agency already has an ad media deal with the brand (known as a media buy). The agency is not willing to disclose the overall agreement currently in place with their client to a network or to an independent producer just to make a new agreement with all of the participants in the deal. Certain things must remain restricted. This requirement must be known and honored.

The new agreement shall therefore only speak in terms of details that are unique to a particular deal.

With agreements, the key thing is to take time to sit with the attorneys and explain the goals of all parties involved. The attorneys must understand the purpose of the business for each of the participating groups. For example, the overall agreement does not have to look like a typical media agreement. The media agreement will only cover what is relevant for the media outlet, the agency, and the brand as it relates to media spots. The importance of content development, the roles, and the responsibilities are not covered in a media deal. A media agreement can be part of an overall branded deal, but a branded deal cannot be "boxed" to fit into a media deal.

THE PITCH

Earlier in this chapter, I talked about the importance of having an idea vetted before turning it into a pitch. If an idea has a solid base and it goes hand in hand with an unfulfilled consumer need, then the idea has a chance to become the anchor of the pitch. The anchor of a pitch can be presented in a multitude of ways. I cannot even begin to suggest how to navigate through the creative process of putting ideas together for entertaining content for the brands because this book does not deal with the creative process, but I can offer pointers that may prove to be helpful when designing a pitch: the key selling points in pitching an entertaining concept with a brand inside. *Important*: Remember that mental preparation is required to prepare for a process that must be successful from the start to continue moving forward. It is one thing to know the steps and quite another to be mentally prepared for how to do it right:

- Make presentation of the idea simple. The idea should be easy to understand and simple to explain.
- Start the presentation with a question that triggers the curiosity of the audience.
- Asking a "what if ..." question is an excellent way to present different scenarios. Use "what ifs" as headers for slides, as long as the "what ifs" help clarify the idea for the audience.
- Use fewer words in visuals than when talking—a lot less. Stand-alone statements do the job. Center each statement on a separate page.
- Images can create vivid mental connections.
- Move toward disclosing the full idea by making an association between two things that are common enough for most people to recognize, e.g., a popular TV show and a sport or well-known personality (e.g., "The Amazing Race Meets the NFL"). The TV show should be one that many people watch or at least have heard about. Most people have watched *The Amazing Race*. If not, they have at least heard about it. Then choose a popular sport or personality who also has a large TV audience. Almost everyone knows about MLB and the NFL. Each correlates with a particular message, but when linked together they provide a stronger visual connection to the idea you are trying to pitch. (For more ideas, research popular programs/series and see how they were explained at first.)

Once the idea is presented, a smooth transition can be made to the *logline* of the idea pitch. The logline is the idea explained in one or two simple sentences. The logline is the centerfold of the pitch. If the idea pitch cannot be understood through the logline, then you probably have not come up with the right logline.

Once common associations and the logline have been designed to capture your audience, the idea pitch follows with a simple description of the concept. The concept describes in more detail what the content idea is intended to do as a solo piece or as a series. Describing the content idea in more detail is not to be confused with development of a *treatment*. The treatment will be developed once the pitch has made progress and received enough positive feedback to continue. *Note*: The only expansion of the concept idea I would suggest could occur when it is time to move to brand integration examples and the concept idea turns into a branded content idea. In this scenario, attaching some content ideas with specific example integrations of the brand may prove to be very useful to bring the pitch "to life."

Brand integrations can be divided into two types: active and passive (Figure 4.5). *Active integrations* occur when the brand is one of the characters. Association of the brand with the content is so strong that the brand takes on a proactive role within the plot. The development of the branded content is carried out by the purpose of the brand. Sometimes the brand is not even seen but is understood by the viewers. The content is intended to have an aftereffect even if the content is nowhere near the viewer. (Remember the example in Chapter 2? A new innovative key for an automobile brand was presented in an episode as a surprise gift to the main character. The unique-looking key was seen and featured

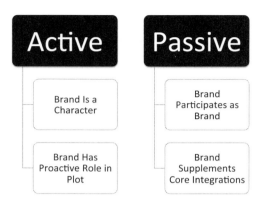

Figure 4.5. Types of Branded Entertainment integrations.

in such unique manner by the main character that the key would later be easily recognized by any viewer and pleasantly remembered on a more personal level.)

Passive integrations occur when the brand participates as a brand by revealing its more obvious side to viewers, e.g., the logo, a tagline, or the product itself is used by one of the characters or placed in a scene. (Passive integration has been referred to as *product integration* in the past.) In the case of Branded Entertainment deals, passive integrations are meant to supplement core integrations: the active ones. Passive integrations are not intended to "bring to life" a branded deal by themselves—this is the biggest difference between product integration and Branded Entertainment. Passive integrations initiate and conclude a deal with simple, somewhat obvious brand inclusion. In Branded Entertainment, brand integration within content is intended to provide well-rounded

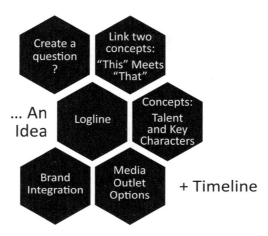

Figure 4.6. Key points to address when preparing a pitch for a content idea.

participation from the brand's perspective. Brand-explicit exposure is not the main purpose inside active integrations.

A pitch can end with some research that opens the possibilities of where the idea can reside in terms of media outlets. If the idea is time sensitive, provide a timeline when an answer is needed.

In summary, key points to address when preparing the pitch of an idea include (Figure 4.6):

- The idea: Use a sentence or a question that includes the idea.
- "This" meets "that:" Describe an association of two concepts that when linked provide the audience with a vivid visual of the idea (e.g., "Sex and the City Meets Dr. Ruth").
- Logline: Use a simple sentence that tells about the content.

- Concept: Develop a paragraph that describes the contour (the general form or structure) of the content (e.g., briefly mention the talent and key characters).
- Brand integrations: Use active or passive forms.
- Potential media outlets: Provide media outlets to approach with the idea.
- Timeline: Provide a timeline for moving forward.

THE PROPOSAL

The previous section is the lead-in to proposal development. Reaching the phase of proposal development means the pitched idea was generally well received even though questions may still come up and suggestions will most likely be made to fine tune the idea to match it to a larger vision. The larger vision is seeing the idea in the context of what it can do for both the brand and the wide audience of the media outlet. Everyone looking at the idea has thoughts as to how the idea will materialize. The key thing at this point is to make sure everyone starts to synchronize their opinions into one central idea. Synchronizing opinions into a central idea requires asking questions to better understand what everyone is thinking about. Realigning everyone's thoughts and restating what the central idea will be is of utmost importance to develop a good proposal.

Content. The proposal is the "meat" of a deal—a natural expansion of the creation and execution of the idea. Providing more detail about how the content will unfold is helpful. The details are considered to be the structure of the proposal. Is the structure short-form (3 minutes or less), mid-form (11 to 13 minutes), or long-form content (44 to 46 minutes)? Is the structure an OTO proposition (one time only for 1 or 2 hours)? Is the structure a series (multiple episodes)? If so, how many episodes—an entire season of 13 episodes or a partial season of possibly 6 episodes? The details regarding how the idea will take form are the structural part of the proposal. Laying the elements out clearly to understand later how a financial model will be built according to the size of the agreement is crucial. This statement does not mean that several options cannot also be offered. One option could be a content series in half hours (11 to 13 minutes) or in full hours (44 to 46 minutes). A somewhat new option is to have both short- and long-form versions of the same content. These options are intended to serve all screens (TV, tablets, web, and mobile). Different versions of the same content can be executed differently depending on the target screens.

Media interest. Determining the structure of the content leads to the financials of the proposal. I strongly suggest that by the time numbers are committed to a proposal that you have a sense of the potentially interested media outlets. If a media outlet is already involved, get a sense of how this media outlet rates in the market against its competitors. Why is knowing how the media outlet rates against its competitors so important? Ratings can be a deal breaker for a brand. A brand or agency will value a Branded Entertainment deal differently based on the suggested platform because of network/platform coverage: the overall popularity and target audience reached most.

Note: I will explain how to best tackle the issue of deal valuation, depending on who leads the overall branded deal, in Chapter 5. This variety of deals with different creative and financial value is one of the reasons why I strongly suggest offering multiple options in the pitch and the proposal—multiple creative options for the right idea and multiple scenarios for the right "home" where the content will "live." By having multiple creative options, the chances of making the best decision for the overall deal improve greatly.

The budget. When content structure and the potential platforms have been determined, it is time to move on to determining the money needed to bring the proposal to fruition. How much "oil" is needed to move the "wheels" of the proposal forward?

Note: I could write several chapters covering different scenarios about how determining the amount of money required can be approached, but truthfully, I would rather give you standard procedures and leave you with the opportunity to create your own procedures over and above these standard procedures. As I said in Chapter 2, I have not had any two deals that were structured exactly alike. Each negotiation had a different approach to how the dollar amounts were gathered to reach a branded deal. Providing simple standard procedures, however, should help demystify how branded deals are really made. These simple standards can serve as a foundation or a template that can be expanded to create more possibilities in the Branded Entertainment field. As a standard procedure in developing a budget, include a detailed section disclosing the total amount needed to create the content. Several scenarios can be presented in this section, depending on the creative options chosen. Choose to be very detailed or to offer a range. I like using ranges because things tend to "mutate" at this stage. Because more things could be added and new ideas might be brought up, ranges seem to fit well in the overall picture. Using a range also provides a safety net until the deal is ready to be completely approved. As approval time approaches, a final detailed budget must be disclosed to all relevant parties. This section must disclose profit margins from parties involved. Be ready to explain why each party is entitled to make the suggested amounts or percentages included in the budget.

The workflow timeline. The next section should be a workflow schedule based on an appropriate timeline for production. Include the preproduction, production, and postproduction schedules. Again, this workflow schedule does not have to be exact, only approximate. Keep in mind that the dates will keep moving until the date when a completed agreement has been fulfilled. (I prefer to include in the workflow all dates when the parties signed their respective agreements. Including the workflow schedule is a helpful tool to get all parties committed to the overall schedule).

Media support. Last but not least is the media support section. The media support section is important because it involves the participation and approvals of several of the parties included in the branded deal. This section contains the media plan that will support all efforts being made to succeed on what has been envisioned. The media plan can include but is not limited to: promotions, traditional spot buys, media relations, official launch strategies, etc. This section also includes the budget needed to execute, but again, the budget needs the participation of more parties: the agency (if involved) and the media outlet. These parties also specify what is needed.

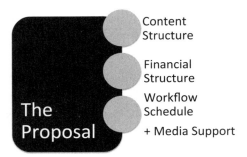

Figure 4.7. Key points to address when preparing a proposal for a content idea.

In summary, the proposal is an important phase in the development process. Key points to address in a proposal include (Figure 4.7):

- Content structure: Provide options (if available) and define the content to be short-, mid-, or long-term, OTO, or a series.
- Financial structure: Include a budget that lays out the dollars needed to produce and execute the idea.
- Workflow schedule: Include the dates to finalize all agreements followed by preproduction, production, and postproduction schedules.
- Media support: Include all media efforts for the content being created. Participation of multiple parties is strongly suggested. A budget is needed for this section, but it may or may not be included in the proposal. The decision is left to the sole discretion of the participants.

THE PAPERWORK

If everything you have done so far has gone well and the parties are ready to formalize the deal, it is time to draft the paperwork. The moment to rejoice with excitement is almost here—almost but not until all parties have inked the deal.

Now comes the part that has earned a bad reputation. Some call this part "the ugly part" because all of the details have not been covered during the earlier stages. When creative juices are flowing and ideas are being presented, everyone seems to be on a high. No one wants to ruin the party with the details. When you have been part of the experience of leaving a meeting after making a successful pitch, and you know the brand loved the idea, no one wants to interrupt the excitement by asking, "But what about …"—the feelings are too good to let go of during these precious moments. As always happens, however, the day will arrive when preliminary discussions have gone well and the parties are ready to draft the paperwork to formalize the relationship. (That is the day when I am reminded that despite my predisposition for "heaven being in the planning," sometimes "the devil in the details" just has to get his due.) The paperwork outlines what each party is responsible for providing and what each party is to receive from the deal (Figure 4.8).

What the Network (Media Outlet) Provides

The network must commit to a programming strategy. When will the content air? What is the time period? What will be the promotional package attached to the content? Will there be any other types of extensions (web-based, mobile, social media)? Is talent part of the deal? Does the network provide in-house talent? If so, who drafts the agreement with the

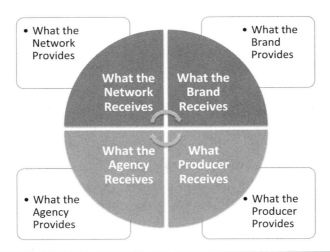

Figure 4.8. Details to include when drafting paperwork.

in-house talent? What ratings commitment can the network offer against the content?

What the Network (Media Outlet) Receives

The network needs details about the content. What are they getting? What is the total package: number of episodes, length, deliverables, and production details in case the network participates in the production process? The network also needs to know their part of the financials of the deal. Is a media buy attached to the deal?

What the Brand (With/Without an Agency as a Mediator) Provides

The brand is the epicenter of a Branded Entertainment deal. Knowing the financial structure of the brand is necessary. The brand can be the full financier of content or a partial funder. Either way, money matters are a big item that must be detailed by the brand. Who gets paid directly? Does the network get the money? Does the money go through an agency? What if the brand pays a producer directly and then the producer buys time from a media outlet? In this case, what are the brand requirements of the media? What is the brand's message? What is on the brand's wish list in terms of integrations? What will the brand commit to in terms of product to be used for the production of content? How do the logistics work from the brand's side? Does the brand provide talent? If so, does the brand do a deal with the talent?

What the Brand (With/Without an Agency as a Mediator) Receives

The brand receives deliverables from multiple sources. The deliverables must be clear from the start:

- From the network, the brand receives:
  - Ratings and marketing information; post-air-date data
  - Access to additional marketing and promotional extensions that involve consumer engagement
  - Public relations initiatives
- From production, the brand receives:
  - Details on the production schedule
  - Details on the integrations: creative suggestions and length
  - Script drafts
  - Postproduction revisions (referred to in the business as "notes"): how many passes; what can or cannot be changed at postproduction time?
  - Creative say and how much?

What Production (Independent or as Part of a Network) Provides

Production is basically an independent entity with producers who will execute the assigned production. Production can also be an in-house division of a media outlet or an agency (pros/cons of in-house producers will be discussed in Chapter 5). Production provides:

- A detailed budget with production fees
- A full production schedule (preproduction, production, and postproduction)
- Creative details of active and passive integrations of the brand
- An approval system (a logistical map to coordinate with the brand/agency and network)
- Talent do's and don'ts regarding the brand
- Cash flow and budget details with appropriate timelines for cash infusions
- Credentials
- The bible table of contents (the "recipe" for how to do the content material) and the dates for submission of other deliverables

What Production Receives

- The "green-light" process spelled out
- Approval process guidelines
- Budget OKs
- Payment chart with date specifications
- A list of executives in charge of production from other parties involved

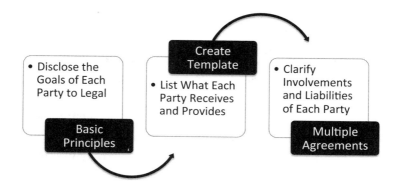

Figure 4.9. Essential legal paperwork for a successful Branded Entertainment deal outlining the legal goals, what each party receives and provides, and the basic principles about the responsibilities and liabilities of each party.

- A list of sideline productions for marketing purposes (webisodes, promos, behind the scenes, bloopers, etc.)
- Deliverable requirements from the media outlet and brand

Legal Essentials

Well-prepared legal paperwork is crucial for a good Branded Entertainment deal to succeed. Legal paperwork outlines the basic principles of the responsibilities and liabilities to each party (Figure 4.9). Even if these principles do not come together under one agreement, they still need to exist and be part of one of the agreements being signed. All parties hold big pieces of the puzzle. All parties have a lot at stake. Everyone has a lot to gain. The degree to which each party is held accountable or benefits from the endeavor must be clearly stated in the paperwork. Key items to address in all paperwork include:

- Disclosure of the goals of each party to legal
- The willingness to create a template from scratch for the deal
- The requirement of more than one agreement to get binding commitments from all parties.
- Inclusion of a list of what each party receives and what each party provides
- A degree of involvement and liability for all parties in the agreements—the brand, the network, the agency, and the production company are involved—no exceptions

As you can see, a lot of information must be disclosed and received. I have chosen to outline these requirements in list form by participating parties to leave the decision of how many agreements are required to the discretion of the deal group. These lists are extremely helpful for checkmarking items that need to be included contractually in binding agreements.

DEAL EXAMPLES

I can recall examples of deals that were structured quite differently from one another. Two of them will be described.

Deal Example 1

An agency was eager to lead a branded deal for their client (a major automotive brand). The agency approached me as the producer. Then together we went and pitched the idea to a global network. After the network was on board, we all pitched the idea to the brand. When it was time to draft the paperwork, the network requested two separate deals: one with the agency (representing their brand) and one with the producer. As the producer, I could not participate in the agency/network deal. After the agreements were concluded, the agency only disclosed to me the do's and don'ts. The guidelines to proceed were based on what was agreed upon in their undisclosed agreement. This deal took almost a year to conclude. The good news is that after success on the air, the network and the brand renewed for another two seasons. Each subsequent year, I took the original templates of each agreement and followed them. The renewal process took only 3 months.

Deal Example 2

A brand approached my production company to rethink their existing arrangement with a network. The brand had a deal in place wherein the network produced the content. The brand was dissatisfied with the quality and core idea the network had been trying to implement. The brand wanted me to present a new idea, build it into a Branded Entertainment concept, and present it to the media outlet as part of the brand's existing media buy with the network. In this scenario, the brand was familiar with my work and was somewhat frustrated with the production quality and central idea of the network content. Before canceling out all efforts on the content, the brand decided to take a chance on an independent production company. (This scenario is ideal for an independent producer because having the brand "on your side" is the most direct way to communicate creativity and manage funds.) In this case, I had an independent deal for the production costs with the brand directly. The brand also had a separate agreement with the network, inclusive of the media buy that was scheduled to support the content. This deal also included a negotiated time schedule, a promotion schedule, and air dates for the series. Production was held responsible under their agreement with the brand to provide the network with support material for promotions and social media conduits. This deal also declared the deliverables to be supplied to the network. At the end, the network was pleased with the results and the brand received what they asked for. This success meant 3 years of renewals.

CHAPTER 5

Leading
the Deal

Previous chapters have provided a foundation for this chapter which will discuss different leadership scenarios when initiating a branded deal. It is important to understand who the players are to have a better perspective of each party's incentives to instigate a branded deal and, equally necessary, to grasp how the process works as the deal gets assembled. In previous chapters, we discussed how a deal starts with an idea. This idea then evolves into a pitch. Then the team puts together a proposal for approval (Figure 5.1). Approval then turns into an agreement comprised of paperwork that details each party's liabilities and responsibilities (Figure 5.2). A standardized Branded Entertainment agreement can be a combination of multiple contracts.

By now, it should be clear that a "cookie cutter" factory approach is not applicable in the evolving business of Branded Entertainment. If you purchased this book expecting to find only one formula for structuring Branded

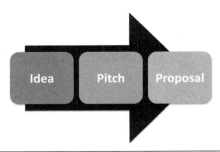

Figure 5.1. Assembly of a deal: first an idea that evolves into a pitch and then into a proposal to be approved.

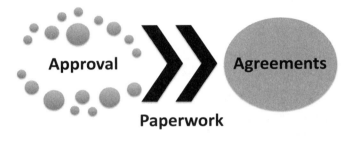

Figure 5.2. Approval of the proposal turns into an agreement with paperwork detailing the liabilities and responsibilities of each party. An agreement can have multiple contracts.

Entertainment deals, from personal experience I can tell you that structuring a Branded Entertainment deal is not as simple as just using a formula or template! The biggest challenge I have encountered over the years was not having *any* template to follow. Many deals later, I realized that each branded agreement had a reason to be as unique as it was. Experience, however, did lead me to simplify the possibilities of deal leadership into three categories.

Figure 5.3. Leadership roles in a branded deal.

The deal itself will not be discussed in this chapter. (Each chapter so far has revealed more and more elements to consider when assembling a deal. Just remember at this point that a deal is assembled as a process, a step-by-step process). Instead I will explore several options for how a deal can be ignited and the nature of the leading role of the party who decides to "move the ball forward." Moving the deal forward is a leadership process—the engine that drives everything else. The different methods in which a deal can be started can be envisioned in three scenarios. Once you understand these options, you will be well on your way to being a part of the short list of people who can honestly be called "closers"—the dealmakers in Branded Entertainment.

Be very aware that the most challenging aspect in assembling a branded deal is not the time consumed but the people you will work with (Figure 5.3). People are the biggest challenge. With this caution in mind, take with it some simple words of wisdom: Pick your partners well!

FORMULA 1: THE AGENCY/BRAND LEADS

Let's start with an ideal case scenario. A brand is interested in becoming a leader in a category or in meeting an under-served consumer need. The brand managers understand the importance of doing marketing in an out-of-the-box way. Branded Entertainment has been identified as a potential solution. Most large brands have an agency of record. Brands may even have more than one agency serving different roles in their overall marketing strategy. The fact that agencies and brands "go together" in so many cases is primarily why these two parties can be merged into one formula to create this scenario. In the Formula 1 scenario, let's assume one agency is leading the process for the brand and the brand is eager to see what possibilities will arise from creating content. With this in mind, the first directive is *immerse yourself in the brand.*

Brand immersion. This type of immersion means to go deep into the research process of what the brand's objectives are, how the brand has accomplished these objectives so far, and what ideal positioning of the brand would be among consumers (Figure 5.4). Other levels of immersion are to understand who the brand's competitors are and how these competitors approach the marketplace. Brand immersion allows us to find the true goals of the brand. These goals can then be paired up with content creation opportunities, including the possibility of owning the content in its entirety.

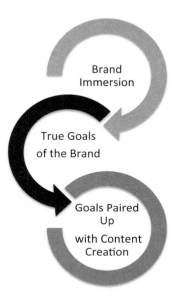

Figure 5.4. Brand immersion allows finding the true goals of a brand that can then be paired with content creation opportunities.

Present the idea. Once the idea takes form based on some possible content options, the idea is then presented to the brand. This idea should target the brand's unfulfilled needs—which is why reaffirming the goals of the brand as the branded content idea is initially introduced to the brand leaders is so important. The point is to show the brand a greater vision of the possibilities as the brand comes into contact with the idea. If the brand can see what the idea can do or how far it can go, then the next level of execution can take place.

Set a budget. The next level of execution requires setting a budget to support the idea and providing options for the media platforms based on how the idea is envisioned and how it will be carried out.

Important to mention at this point is if the brand has more than one agency, the leading agency will have to incorporate the other agencies into the process (a small, but crucial detail). Nowadays, a single brand typically enlists more than one agency. These agencies must work together throughout the Branded Entertainment process because these counterpart agencies may be directly responsible for key roles in the process: roles such as creativity, planning, and media buying. Each area of agency responsibility will have a place in the overall deal. Each agency can also be instrumental in gaging how much money is needed to make the deal happen. Once the idea has taken shape, has been preapproved by the brand, and all other agencies are up to speed on what comes next, the meeting with the network takes place. (*Note:* At this point, numerous meetings between the brand and the lead agency have already taken place. Both the brand and the lead agency have been sold on making the deal happen if all things align well with a content outlet.)

Meet with the network. Next is to determine the mission of the initial branded team (which can be comprised of one or more agency members and possibly a brand champion). At the meeting with the network, the goal of the branded team is to ensure that the vision of the brand is aligned with the central purposes of the branded deal. Ensuring alignment of the vision with the central purposes of both the brand and the network is at the center of the equation. Starting network meetings at the programming level (if possible) is best. In a best-case scenario, network meetings should be with the top level of programming or content development. If the network likes the idea and the overall structure of what the deal could be, then some brainstorming on refining the creative concepts previously covered at the initial meeting will take place. This step should be used to further enhance the overall branded content idea. Media platforms and networks know their audiences quite well and can bring instrumental ways to execute and promote new content to the table. If the chemistry is right between the parties of a deal of this nature, this can be the time when the network might decide to add a member to the branded team. Adding a member to the team is usually at the network's discretion because this member must serve as an internal liaison with the network. (*Note*: The network/platform selection process, if needed, can be repeated with multiple contenders until certainty is reached about who the best network partner should be.)

Financials. The next part of the process is when/if the network/media platform incorporates ad sales into the conversations. The ad sales group will discuss the current spending status of the brand with the branded team if the brand is a current client. Then media support dollars for the branded deal are discussed in the hope of raising the overall level of investment of the brand within the network. Figures can be presented in percentages, not actual currency, if a high level of confidentiality is required. (This is only when multiple parties are present at this meeting. Later on, specific figures will have to be revealed to the brand.) This portion of the branded deal's budget falls under media support/financials on the proposal. The production budget included under financials for content creation is separate and independent from the media support dollars. The ad sales division from a media platform needs to be sold on the idea as much as their counterparts in the programming department are. Ad sales have an extra incentive. In addition to an extra media buy from the brand, ad sales may be able to retain a certain number of minutes to sell to other advertisers and generate even more incremental revenue. Now it becomes clear to all involved that part of the agreement when the brand/agency leads the way is that the overall deal includes a "suggested media buy." This will surround the airtime of the newly created branded content. In addition to the media buy, the number of minutes available inside the new content can and should be negotiated with the network. If the network/media platform is not contributing some real dollars toward the overall production, then the brand/agency's job is to retain sufficient minutes to commercialize later on and add these minutes to the profit center of the deal. The idea behind asking for money from the media platform is because the media also have annual spending budgets for creating new content. A branded content idea is considered to be new content. The financial variables should be discussed at length to avoid a short-lived deal or a one-winner scenario.

The deal. Typically, the deal is between the agency and the network/media platform. This deal may look similar to a media deal, but it is not. Contingencies are attached to the deal to comply with the cash infusions necessary throughout the production. These cash infusions can include the overall budget for production. Attached to the deal can be the terms of the deal between the leading agency and the team responsible for producing the content, the deliverables regarding quality, and product exposure. Last but not least is the deal between the brand and its agency. This deal can be as simple as a one-time-only branded deal or adding an addendum to an existing agreement.

Establish a payment plan. The network then has to agree to a payment plan that is in line with the production cash flow timeline should the network decide not to produce the content in-house. Production always depends on cash infusions, even as early as the preproduction stage.

Some benefits of an agency/brand lead include:

- The network/media platform gains by having overall ad spending sweetened by a moderate increase in the brand's spending level or by the addition of a brand that is new to their current client roster.
- The leading agency gets the credit for having brought to life a more innovative marketing strategy, an incentive that may include content ownership.
- The brand gets at least partial ownership of an idea that can be multiplied on various media fronts if played correctly. In the eyes of consumers of these brands, what these brands do is considered to be different and revolutionary—game changers. A deal like this does not need to be limited to one "playground." The deal can also be expanded into other markets and media platforms.

FORMULA 2: THE NETWORK LEADS

Developing fresh innovative programming ideas at the network level is no longer commonplace, even though such an imperative is still placed on the networks. Gaps in what may be missing content-wise might not be so obvious to those who labor inside the ever-changing world of media. In this environment, a Branded Entertainment deal can offer a timely opportunity for a network or a media outlet. The opportunity could be due to a particular gap in a time period within the programming grid or caused by a target audience that is not being reached properly. Competitors may also be programming more aggressively toward a new audience. These situations are just some of the common examples that trigger a *head start*, a network/media platform having a leadership role in a Branded Entertainment deal.

Note: As I discuss the network lead type of deal formula, I will refer to any or all media outlets that could fall under the category as *networks*—media outlets such as over-the-air broadcasters, cable networks, and all forms of digital media platforms. I would also like to point out that the possibility of a network deciding to produce its own branded production internally is real. Even so, the need to form allies early on and build a combined branded team is important to secure additional funding. Partners bring good things to the table. Sometimes "sharing cookies" in the process ultimately gets everyone more cookies at the end.

Consider an independent producer. If a network chooses to start out solo, the efforts to carry out a branded deal may seem confusing for other parties in the deal. The deal has the danger of being perceived as an effort to create just another elaborate media deal with a brand. Over the course of time, I have noticed that what seems to work best is to secure an independent production company that understands each party's involvement from the start. Choosing this type of independent production company serves two purposes:

- An independent neutral party can understand the real needs of the network. (An outside neutral party may be able to see what many on the inside cannot.)
- The brand can sense the effort to have a greater degree of fairness in the entire process. (The brand, however, will always be guarded throughout the creative process.)

Assemble the team. At this point, the branded team can be assembled to work on the branded content idea—but not in a vacuum. This initial team may have one or two members from the network and one additional member from the production company. Listening to the network is next. Part of the listening process includes understanding the puzzle regarding how to best reach the audience and getting a "dream list" from the network: what elements does the network want to have inside the branded content (e.g., one of their own hosts)? Then, listen to what is available in terms of resources such as cash and other bargaining items. The network may have a small amount of cash allocated for new endeavors. The question of alternative resources becomes fundamental at this early stage. Is the network willing to see this idea come to fruition as a co-production? If so, potential partners could either be an agency, a brand, a production company, or some combination of these three. A co-production could provide several opportunities in a branded deal (Figure 5.5):

Figure 5.5. Co-production opportunities in a branded deal.

- A financial commitment: Ownership can be joint, with the parties having similar rights to the newly created content. Distribution and syndication rights are also included for both.
- Co-creation rights: All parties can add to the idea. All parties need and want to carry out the fulfillment of their goals within the overall purpose of the branded deal.
- Future leadership: Shared lessons from early branded experiences can pay off at a later time.

Note: I am a believer in building in "outs" for the parties in a deal in case one of the parties decides to move on. If one of the parties does not want to continue with the deal or wants to change strategies, the deal should not cease to exist. The deal should have a plan for how the parties can part ways. The remaining partner(s) could bring a new partner to the table and continue creating a future deal. The network might not want to continue the deal, but the same deal might be of great interest to a new media outlet such as a web platform.

Research the brand. Next comes planning and research. Let's assume the network prefers a brand. The branded team pulls out any and all information regarding "brand intel." The plan is for the network to have a working understanding of what the brand is seeking. The goal is to make this scenario a simultaneous discovery—for the brand and the network.

Consider risk sharing. The scenario wherein a network leads a branded deal is very common. In today's marketplace, the landscape makes having another partner with whom to share risks almost fundamental. If a network is willing to co-author something new, the reality is simple—dollars are needed to make the deal come through. The mission is to find a partner with a similar dream and create a partnership for a branded deal. An independent producer might want to participate, for instance.

Make the pitch. The pitching of the idea will be to the brand managers and the agency, if required. (The procedure discussed in Chapter 4 still needs to be followed—the pitch, then the proposal.) If both parties see eye to eye on the idea, then an agreement can be reached and the necessary paperwork can be drafted.

Financials. The financial structure of a network-lead deal is usually consistent with the interest level of each party. Ideally, each party contributes a similar amount of dollars. Then, the proportion of dollars plays into future gains and extended distribution possibilities. The branded team maintains the integrity of having a financially balanced deal across all participating parties to make it a win-win deal.

Some benefits of the network-lead formula include:

- The network is already a key participant from the start. There is immediate power in exposing new content to an audience the network understands well.
- The brand's perspective is most likely positive. The brand is "on board" if the branded content is right for them.
- As the leading partner, the network usually likes to see these ventures from a long-term perspective. An understanding of what it takes for new content undertakings is already in place.
- The future exploitation of new content may be easier to execute because most media platforms already have a specialized arm that handles the monetization process.

FORMULA 3: THE CONTENT DEVELOPER/ PRODUCER LEADS

Although highly rewarding, the scenario of a content developer/producer lead is the most work-intensive of all. Simply put, the basics of this scenario are more complex. The producer/independent producer also does all the work in bringing in and convincing several powerhouse partners to join the party! (*Note*: For purposes of discussing this category in greater detail, the term *producer* includes production companies, independent producers, content developers, and content consultants.)

Producers must have a good understanding of the marketplace. This understanding can be attained by researching the consumer world: the trends, habits, and tendencies of different generations. Understanding can also be gained from relationships in the media industry. Agencies, brands, and networks are good "storytellers" regarding what is new, what is changing, and what is becoming increasingly more interesting.

The goal of a producer is to understand what is missing in the marketplace. Is there a gap that is not being addressed by anyone? Is there a content format developed in another part of the world that could be of good use on this side of the globe? These are questions that a producer must address before deciding to enter the Branded Entertainment world.

Let's assume a producer is able to identify a need or format that could be successful with a new audience or a new region. The producer's role starts with development of the idea and evolution of a pitch. (*Note:* If the idea involves an existing format, the producer must negotiate in advance any necessary rights needed to present the idea to potential partners.)

Start with the brand managers. Ideally, I suggest starting the process with the brand's leaders: the brand managers. Brand managers are the gate keepers of a brand and obviously are the most important people to get on board because they hold the purse strings. The ideation process around identifying how to bring a brand to life can take multiple forms. An agency can be included in this process. A series of brainstorming sessions with the brand and the agency can help the producer better understand what truly is important

Figure 5.6. Producer options for content ownership.

to the brand. Another way in which the agency can play a pivotal role in branded deals is by bringing additional brands to the table. If additional brands are included in the deal, the agency could share the leadership role with the producer, assembling an agency agreement that includes more than one brand in the content agreement.

Content ownership. The question of content ownership is an important one to address when a producer leads the process. The producer may choose to retain some creative and/or ownership rights and license the rest to the brand and/or the network. Another option for the producer is to have a three-way partnership wherein all parties involved equally share the rights of the creative material. In another scenario, when the producer has no interest in being a content owner, the network and/or the brand can have an agreement called "work for hire." Content ownership is turned over to any of the involved parties. The producer only stands to make a production fee out of the deal (Figure 5.6). More possibilities exist in the rainbow of branded deals, but these are the most common. Two scenarios describe ownership:

- The producer allows the network to make an agreement with the agency and then makes a secondary agreement with the network as the producer of the content. In this scenario, it is feasible that the network will contribute partially to the production budget. If the network contributes to the production budget, the network will share a leading role in the creative process. The producer and the network both have a say. If the network sees a long-term future for the idea, the network can make an offer to the producer to purchase the content idea format outright.

- The brand may be interested in partnering up with the producer. If the brand is very interested in the idea, the brand can make an offer to own the idea outright and have the producer be a work-for-hire party. (*Note*: The brand needs to know where this content will possibly live. Until that point is reached, the brand may hesitate to make a full commitment to the producer.)

Team members. In the early days, many meetings were arranged to first secure a network and then bring the network to the brand as a possible home for the content in question. My approach uses a different strategy: add a brand member to the branded team and bring the brand member to the network meetings to secure more than one option for the brand. This approach has been very inviting to the networks. The networks immediately feel committed to be at this meeting and usually suggest ideas that could complement what is being offered. If the brand is partnered with a growing agency, the brand member can be from the agency team. Remember that agencies have access to all networks. Agencies can be excellent allies for getting into places that a producer may not be able to access easily. One of my most successful deals to date was through an agency champ who would not accept luke-warm responses from obviously interested networks. The agency champ was convinced that the idea had all the signs of success. She took on the mission of making a few calls. She invited me as a producer to present to a network at a meeting I could have not gotten into on my own. She not only got me into the meeting, but a deal was inked, even though the network had given all the "maybes" possible with no certainty of a commitment. In the end, a person inside the network became an internal champion who would not take no for an answer within his company, taking the deal all the way to the top. This branded deal was recognized by *The New York Times* for having the most brands included in a series in which the brands were the "stars" of the show, yet high entertainment value for viewers was maintained. This show was a sports scripted series called *El Diez* (10). Five brands participated: an airline, a fast food company, a beer company, a domestic car company, and a home improvement company.

Some benefits of a producer-lead formula include:

- Parties have true independence and can provide an abundance of ideas.
- Parties have flexibility to partially or totally own an idea.

Leadership Categories

Brand/Agency	Network	Producer
• Brand could get partial ownership • Agency will get creative points for being innovative • Network can get incremental revenue	• Power in exposing audiences to new content • Brand perspective positive from the start • Offers long-term business perspective	• Abundance of ideas and independence to create • Flexibility to partially or totally own the idea • The ideal branded team comes to life

Figure 5.7. Benefits summary of three leadership options: agency/brand, network, and content developer/producer.

- The ideal branded team comes to life. Participants from each party join in. All ideas are entertained throughout the process.
- Producers have access to other producers who could come in and work as a neutral, fair party in the overall deal.

These three formula categories were created in retrospect—after many deals—and looking back, I realized that the mechanics, timing, and each party's involvement were different in each case (Figure 5.7). What became most noticeable was that many deals had some similarities—and those similarities had to do with the party who ignited the deal.

Understanding the significance of who takes the leadership role and what that means to everyone involved is crucial

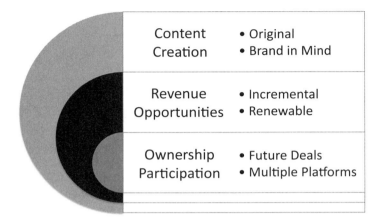

Content Creation	• Original • Brand in Mind
Revenue Opportunities	• Incremental • Renewable
Ownership Participation	• Future Deals • Multiple Platforms

Figure 5.8. Key benefits for any party leading a Branded Entertainment deal.

to landing Branded Entertainment deals. As long as the formula used includes original content creation with high-level integrations and offers an equal opportunities to share some revenue and some ownership, a Branded Entertainment deal will most likely be well on the way to happening (Figure 5.8).

CHAPTER 6

Money

Money is the oil needed to move the wheels of a proposal forward. Money is also the horse that pulls the Branded Entertainment wagon. This wagon can seat a number of participants, but it takes money to move the wagon wheels forward. Branded Entertainment deals are by definition unique, but how they are funded makes branded deals especially distinct. The issue of funding is probably one that deserves the most explaining. I am often asked this question: "Just tell me who funds the deal—is it the advertiser or is it the network?" Sources of money and how deals are funded deserve a full chapter because multiple parties and different possibilities are involved.

Money in the branded content context concerns funding and profit. Without funding partners, a Branded Entertainment deal stands very little chance of making it off the ground. Without profit, chances are a deal will only last for the short run. In this context, important points to grasp are how to secure a level of investment from one or more potential parties and how to make sure everyone included is

Funding

- Who funds the deal?
- How much funding is needed?
- Can funding be shared?

Profit

- What is the expected revenue?
- Can the revenue be diversified?

Figure 6.1. Money in branded content matters: funding and compensation.

compensated for their participation. These points are probably the trickiest pieces of the puzzle to solve because the formula for determining investment levels and compensation for the participants is not simple (Figure 6.1).

The single most important question that I am asked by agencies, brands, networks, and producers is: "Where did you get the money to do this?" The follow up question is then: "And how did you do it?" Fully understanding the many possible answers to the questions about investment and compensation is crucial because being creative and innovative in the funding process can close a deal that might not otherwise get off the ground.

Let's go back to the basic concept of what Branded Entertainment is. The nature of Branded Entertainment implies that a brand partially or fully funds a content-related deal. This implication, in and of itself, tells us that brands will take a leading role in the funding process. The issue is whether the brand looks for the funding alone or from others. If the brand is willing to consider other partners, then the mix of funding sources grows. Other partners to be considered are the media networks and the producers/creators of

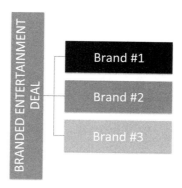

Figure 6.2. A Branded Entertainment deal with 1+ brands.

the idea at hand—and yes, doing a branded deal with more than one brand for the same content is possible (Figure 6.2).

By the time one or more parties are interested in possibly funding a deal, it is time to focus on how much money is required to get the deal in place. Once the money requirement is outlined, the profits should be estimated. Last, but not least, the way this all comes together is via procedures that are in place that structure cash inflow and outflow. Money transactions in Branded Entertainment deals can be outlined as follows (Figure 6.3):

- Cash infusion: Money as an investment to secure the branded deal
- Profit imperatives: Money as profit to all participating parties
- Money management: Systems designed to monitor a newly designed multitier deal

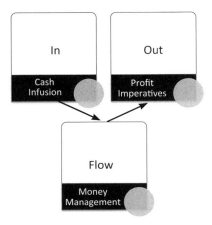

Figure 6.3. Money transactions outline in a Branded Entertainment deal.

CASH INFUSION

Think of what is needed to produce content. One of the first things that comes to mind is cash, isn't it? More often than not the need for cash is either first or second to the actual idea. A Branded Entertainment deal is no different than any other media deal—cash is required to create and execute a deal. The big question is: "Who pays the bills?" Historically speaking, ever since audiences have come together to be entertained, there has been a need to produce content to do so. For as long as there has been content to produce, there have been parties willing to pay for it—which is why millions of hours of entertaining content have been produced day after day to fulfill the entertainment needs of millions of viewers/consumers. Traditionally speaking, it is safe to assume that the paying (cash) party that first comes to mind is the network—the media outlets.

Let's review the Branded Entertainment concept. The concept puts the brand at the center of the table—the epicenter of the deal. Having said this, the produced entertainment must be engaging for a deal to work. Engaging brand content means creating a symbiotic relationship in which both the brand and the content need each other to survive. One does not go in front of the other. Brand and content walk together in the creative process, which is a crucial premise to understand as we approach the question of funding as a mechanism to put a deal in place.

The cash infusion envisioned to cover all angles of content production is a black and white proposition, but who participates in the funding deal is not. A branded deal can be robustly funded in different ways, mostly depending on how the business side of the branded deal is structured. If the content to be created presents opportunities to flourish in more ways than just capturing eyeballs, a deal may be open to having more than one funding entity.

The Brand as the Funding Party

Let's start with the brand being the sole funding entity. For a brand, there are countless ways to participate in media. The majority of options a brand is presented with are traditional. For example, an ad campaign is required by brand X. A promise of delivering potential consumers is made by a media outlet Y. Then, the value of the media deal is determined by a formula that includes the frequency of exposure of the ad and the reach of the potential target audience brand X is seeking. Further evolution of these deals includes non-traditional ad campaigns and marketing strategies that are

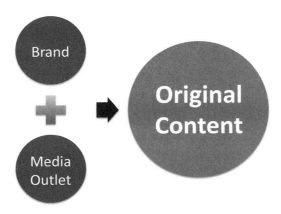

Figure 6.4. Creativity as top of mind in Branded Entertainment.

more of a *guerilla* style in which the goal becomes reaching consumers in a nontraditional way.

Branded Entertainment has become a part of the evolution of media deals, but it's more than that. A better way to explain this situation would be to say that Branded Entertainment is the return of brand participation inside the content (Figure 6.4). From television's earliest years, brands came "along with" the content—both sharing a common goal to reach consumers by the masses. In essence, brands and entertaining content have been together from before the start of television, even going back to the days of radio and the earliest recognition of patrons for supporting the arts.

New is the restructuring of deals with a brand wherein creativity is "top of mind." The creativity seeks to not distort the core of any content, but only to blend in. By blending in, consumers relate to both the entertainment value and the emotional attachment to the brand. Today, media outlets in

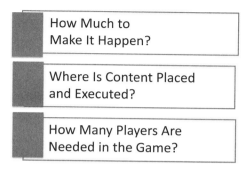

How Much to
Make It Happen?

Where Is Content Placed
and Executed?

How Many Players Are
Needed in the Game?

Figure 6.5. Contributors to the money formula.

general speak to a more "evolved" consumer. Evolved consumers are far more savvy than they used to be—not only
back in the early days of television but also just a decade ago.
Living in an era where multi-screens rule, having creative,
innovative, and engaging content is the "new black" so to say.
This evolved process, which results in the creation of blended
content, is much more demanding on creators. The goal is to
optimize creativity to a degree in which a brand is engaged
without interfering in the content and is incapable of "turning off" the viewer's "volatile" engagement—their ability to
easily switch to something else if they are not getting what
they want. To viscerally understand this relationship is to
know the *how* of Branded Entertainment.

So why are we discussing creativity in a chapter that is
to only deal with money? The reason I am emphasizing the
creative aspect of the deal in this chapter is because creativity
is where the money needs to go. If a brand is the sole funding entity, the brand has to consider the process of creativity,
proper execution, and other contributing factors (Figure 6.5).

These considerations are the three drivers of money. Contributors to the money formula are:

- How much money is needed to make the creativity happen?
- Where is content placed and executed?
- How many players are needed in the game?

How Much Money Is Needed to Make It Happen?

Probably still unclear to the brand is what type of creativity is being invested in. The investment is in the creative work that assembles a great idea for consumers with the attributes of the brand intertwined within this content. "How much" corresponds to the partial or full expenditure needed to take an idea from its initial stage to the final stage of produced content.

Simple? Not really! The confusion arises when the brand still believes the investment should only go toward amplifying an ad campaign. Amplifying an ad campaign is not the purpose of Branded Entertainment. Creating *inside* content is not the same as creating *around* content. Brands willing to participate inside content have to go through a rigorous process in which the brand's objectives and personality need to match the core concept of the idea. Only then will the branded content not seem like an ad, or look like one, to a consumer, necessities for the full purpose of the content to be realized.

Where Is Content Placed and Executed?

Choosing the right destination for the content is also an investment. Which media or combination of several outlets

Figure 6.6. Options in placement negotiations.

will make the most impact in the eyes of targeted consumers? Having a solid idea blended with the brand and turning it into engaging content is the first step toward a successful Branded Entertainment initiative. The second step is to place this content in one or several media outlets where it can be seen by the right target audience. Placement also requires an investment. Most media outlets require a financial gain in this process. The question is how much. Several options can facilitate placement negotiations (Figure 6.6):

- As an ad campaign surrounding the newly created content
- As an investor and co-producer
- As a "time buy," in which the network rents its space out for a fixed amount of money each time the content airs
- As a barter deal, in which media outlets retain the commercial minutes and later sell them to other advertisers

- As a revenue share deal, in which revenue gathered from other advertisers from the commercial minutes is split among the parties

How Many Players Are Needed in the Game?

Why is it necessary to define the number of players now? The answer is because money plays a big role in deciding how many players should participate. Although money is not the sole factor, it is an important one. Money can be a "deal breaker." When not enough money is on the table to make a funded idea happen, no idea can get off the ground—no matter how great it is.

So, who are the usual suspects to be players? Obvious partners to be brand investors are all media outlets, producers/production companies, and other brands (not competing in the same category). Sometimes governing agencies (e.g., ministries from governmental divisions) and sports leagues can act as the funders of an idea if the content serves a greater purpose for their overall goal. For instance, money can be given by governing entities as an incentive to produce innovative content; then the process is used as a way to transfer knowledge to their local public teams.

Creativity does not follow the "rules" of a media buy when it comes to money. Early on in the process, many brand leaders thought that a Branded Entertainment deal should be valued like an ad buy. I am not saying that a media buy should not accompany a branded deal—only that the pricing and valuations are very different. Media buys can be combined at the end to provide an overall value to the brand, but the considerations to keep in mind before the money is assigned and distributed for the creative Branded Entertainment work are the same as for production.

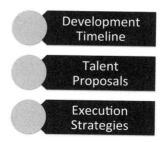

Figure 6.7. Values to include in a budget.

As new content starts the ideation process, there needs to be an understanding that the development of concepts has a value, a monetary value for the overall production. Additionally, if talent is needed for the idea to be executed, the talent also has a value in the budget. The cash value measurement of how much of each "ingredient" goes into a deal can vary greatly depending on the "umbrella" that embraces the deal's overall execution—which is why I encourage production budgets to be "black and white." Budgets demystify one of the greatest enigmas regarding how much funding cash is the "right" amount for a branded deal. Disclosing budgets helps reveal development time, talent proposals, and execution strategies to carry out the entire plan (Figure 6.7).

Some are surprised at first to hear that I recommend full budget exposure when making a cash request, but bear in mind that what is gained by doing it this way is the creation of a template that becomes standard practice for this industry. Full budget exposure serves one enormous purpose: it refutes the idea that a branded deal equals the valuation of an ad campaign measured in seconds of airtime.

Note: In my years of trying different methods to fund a deal, I have come to the conclusion that if a brand is approached, most likely the brand will listen. The key is to get to the brand on a face-to-face basis. Two rules to follow are:

- Approach the right person.
- Present the right ideas.

The Brand as a Co-Funding Party

Now let's continue our discussion with the brand as a co-funding entity. As I mentioned earlier, the structure of the business side of Branded Entertainment deals can trigger the ambitions of other participating parties. This triggering of the ambitions of other parties adds potential for the content to go further and potentially bring new revenue to other entities of the deal: the network and the production.

If the content at hand has potential to live on for more than one episode, one season, or one market, chances are good there are other potential business avenues to explore. The possibilities for growth need to be disclosed as estimates or projections to fully assess the risk/reward for each party. For instance, a network may see the possibility of partially owning the format and replicating it in other markets. Production may see the viability of having subsequent airing windows and selling the content that has been produced in other territories. If the content is good enough, content amplification is definitely a business proposition. Plus, if the brand has a piece of the action, content amplification may translate into an opportunity to share with internal counterparts in other regions and replicate similar deals in other territories.

Even if content amplification is not the case and the brand has no gain in sharing with its counterparts, the format of the content can still function as a business model in which replicas of the format are doable without a brand inside. This scenario continues to be a clear opportunity for the other parties—networks, production entities, and even agencies—to now get very involved in the content ownership business.

In summary, the funding of a deal is proportionate to the opportunity factor for each party involved. I have seen models in which each party shares equally the total funding needed and I have seen models in which the brand puts in 75% with the network picking up the rest. Reducing the overall investment is also a way to participate. I have also seen production entities that participate in the funding by reducing the budget on the development front. All options must be looked at because funding is not easy to assemble. So by proposing a model in which others are let in, a brand can gain partners willing to share the risk of a startup and the others can gain entry into new business opportunities beyond their core.

PROFIT IMPERATIVES

Let's now address why each of the players needs to have "a piece of the action." Profit is to be made all along the way for all parties involved. For example, some stages require a particular skill or asset. The two most common stages requiring special skills or assets are during assembly of the deal and after consummation of the deal. The parties contributing these skills and assets expect to receive payment of a fee or a percentage. Each participating party is due a piece of the money earned. Identify fees or percentages from the overall deal as part of everything being developed and constructed to incentivize all parties and to ensure active engagement at all times.

The Brands

Brands need a return on investment (ROI). ROI can be calculated from a short-term or long-term perspective. Brand managers also look at new opportunities or audiences to expose their brand. This core group of experts inside the brand evaluates different opportunities for growth and will try new things because consumers are harder to get and tougher to keep these days.

Just as content options for viewers have grown exponentially, so have consumer choices for products and services. The old days of explosive ratings are mostly over, as are the days of a brand totally controlling a category. Brand presence and brand profitability are now continuously at risk. Volatility in the market is here to stay. All are signs of the times. Blinking lights signaling opportunity sit across the table from a brand. It is time to act. The traditional way of doing business is quickly becoming obsolete. During a Q&A session at an initial meeting, the brand must give some indication that the current efforts of the brand are not completely fulfilling goals. If the eagerness of the brand to find new ways to increase business is genuine and exploratory, this eagerness could indicate that some "risk" dollars are available to allocate toward new ways to multiply business. The potential of this new business means that Branded Entertainment can become a possible new way to get to the heart of the consumer. In this case, the investment is in emotional engagement, which is what Branded Entertainment is all about.

The profit a brand stands to make in any branded deal can be used to reposition the way the brand finds consumers. When engagement from consumers is strongly linked to content, the brand will most likely benefit. Consumers are so far from passive these days that they can redirect an entire marketing campaign just by showing their friends and the world what they love or hate on social media. Beyond the point of being remembered, a brand now has the potential to stay linked to consumers' hearts and emotional decisions. I think that is the profitable "state of mind" every brand seeks.

When the time comes to measure the results, find out how the brand will measure success. Will success be measured as a percentage over normal expectations? Is success about moving cases or consumer recognition? Are distributors and retailers part of the measuring results process? These metrics will help you analyze and interpret data once the project has finished.

If the ability for a brand to own or co-own content is in the deal, the deal has an opportunity to create new revenue streams and expand profits beyond the brand's own product sales. Related products and merchandising can be linked to the brand and can generate new profit. Shelf space is also a high-caliber commodity. By retaining an association with the right content, any promotional efforts with the brand can also increase the possibilities of multiplying shelf space. What's not to love about that?

The Agencies

Historically agencies have been all about fees. A fee was generated based on the work performed by the agency on behalf of the client, the brand. The fee fluctuated according to the brand's billings. The higher the billings were, the lower the fee was on a percentage basis, but understood was that ultimately the "take home" amount for the agency would increase proportionately as the client invested more in a brand. Those days, however, are nearly gone. The industry has outgrown the traditional model of agency fees. In today's competitive landscape, fees are a luxury that no longer fits in the new standard model. The new game in town is called *results* and compensation is tied to results. If a client discusses fees, the discussion is done with the purpose of obtaining a blanket list of services for a flat amount, a "one-price-fits-all" model.

Abrupt changes from the traditional business model have contributed to the spread of uncertainty across the agency business. As a result, competition has become more ferocious than ever. Survival of the fittest is the current mindset. New services have to be created. These new services are being marketed as "groundbreaking" and "unique" to grow the agency's business. This is a snapshot of what is happening today.

So, where does Branded Entertainment fit in? A well-thought-out Branded Entertainment plan can keep agencies away from the "review abyss." The interesting part of the Branded Entertainment model is that agencies can participate in obtaining a percentage for their contribution to the entire business model, especially if the agency leads the deal. The business development aspect of getting it all together is very important. If an agency plays it right, they can control the brand (to a certain degree). They already control the media outlets. Additionally, the agency can choose which production group to bring in and whether this group comes from inside or outside the agency. Once a deal is sketched out, the agency once again can participate in generating specific creative work that leads to good content development. Once production is underway, the agency may choose to have a line item within the production budget to monitor the process and ensure proper coordination across the board from all parties. The agency holds a unique spot by knowing both a brand's spending levels and also the "pain points" for media outlets. Knowledge of both gives the agency a good sense of what a deal breaker can be.

Crucial is that the agency ensures the Branded Entertainment investment models live "outside the box." I know this sounds clichéd, but the past is the norm (the box). Branded Entertainment deals need to be at a different level. In the case of an agency needing Branded Entertainment to sweeten the pie of a pitch, my suggestion is to leave a small clause for the negotiation of new business opportunities brought to the brand. Branded deals are new business for a brand. They can be staged separately from media/marketing/digital services. In fact, owning content or co-funding a new venture in a branded deal is a distinct offering from the norm. An agency can always leave open the option of adding a line for compensation for services rendered inside the production line as a "line item" of the branded business. As long as all profit is transparent to all participating funding entities, the brand should be okay with agreeing to split the funding according to the values agreed upon in the deal.

The Networks (Media Outlets)

Networks measure profit in overall revenue from different revenue-driven divisions. The revenue that corresponds to this side of the business comes from advertisers. Every year, the measuring factor becomes the overall revenue increase (or decrease). An increase is measured as a percentage over the year prior, taking into consideration overall industry growth providing each media outlet with a market share coming from the overall piece of advertising dollars. This measurement marks the foundation of what the "right number" for revenue should be. This "right number" is considered to be an estimate that is continuously affected by natural competition among networks. Each network wants a piece of their competitor's market share and quite aggressively attempts to take a bite out of it (known as incremental revenue per advertiser).

Meanwhile, on the client's side, advertisers analyze the market with the goal of creating an investment strategy based on particular criteria: target demographics, market size, network/platform coverage, popularity, brand recognition, etc. According to the level of importance of each criterion, networks rank them in order of importance, which allows the advertiser to divide the investment accordingly. (This is just the initial formula.) So how do the networks retain a higher chunk of the overall share of dollars allocated by a brand for marketing/promotion/advertising (known as incremental revenue)? Generating incremental revenue involves Branded Entertainment deals creating an offering far more unique and creative in which the brand gets to play a protagonist role. In return, the brand measures the potential effectiveness of these unique deals differently than traditional advertising, opening the door for incremental revenue to the network willing to explore and diversify.

This explanation is how it all works conceptually. Now, moving the theory to reality implies that internal departments have to be in agreement to follow a different journey and go after the out-of-the-box dollars. Although the ultimate goal is positive, the first natural reaction internally tends to be resistance. Having been an insider and an outsider in the network environment, I have witnessed uphill battles that have defined for me the difference between powerful deals and forceful ones. If the proposed deal comes in forcefully, ignited by one department in which one person dictates the flow, the result (after a long, tiresome process) is that the deal typically does not happen at all or if it does happen, the deal dies shortly after a brief doomed existence. Time and time again I have noticed that if the deal is co-authored by several people based in different network groups, the deal becomes a powerful opportunity that promises success and optimal results.

Profits inside a network can also be measured by the savings originated by these deals. We know for a fact that each programming/content department has a spending goal, a budget, and each dollar contributed by another party is a dollar saved by the programming team. Now we have a scenario in which two in-house departments have a big win. Sales revenue increases by generating a deal that calls for incremental dollars and programming gets to possibly save on content development by having an investment partner.

A network can participate in the profit sharing by adding an ad campaign to the branded deal. This ad campaign must be specific to the idea. The proposal to execute the ad plan successfully should also involve participation by any of the platforms by which the network has reach to the consumer in mind. Another way to participate in the overall profit picture is through the co-development of the idea. Once the idea has been formed, the network can take an ownership share and any further sales on the format or syndication of what has been produced can generate a new source of business for the network.

Another medium- to long-term strategy is to generate new revenue by creating case studies of Branded Entertainment deals and pitch them to brands that are not a part of the current client roster. Rather than proposing the usual media tactics, best may be to start an approach placing content co-creation as the centerfold of a strategy. Adding creative members to the pitching team, for instance, independent creators and authors of previous Branded Entertainment deals, can add a layer of differentiation and credibility regarding what is being proposed.

These branded deals do not re-draft the course of normal business, but they certainly can add something of value to the overall picture of a network. Once a Branded Entertainment deal has been consummated and details are released to the media, industry reporters usually make a point of talking about the deal. This attention brings more bees to the hive.

Note: Again I will state that Branded Entertainment deals are not optimal for all brands. For instance, non-consumer brands such as business-to-business products and some consumer services are not ideal. Retirement funds could be a challenge to fit into content creatively. For those brands that believe in innovation and leadership, however, the Branded

Entertainment approach can offer these brands everything they have been waiting to get from a network.

The ratings game has been the main "ruler" for measuring profitable empires. Today, the ratings game is ever changing. Ratings are no longer part of the formula for how brands choose to spend marketing dollars on distribution platforms and networks. Profits for media outlets on an annual basis are no longer guaranteed based on pure ratings performance. Competition has never been so wide and vast. Each platform gets a new competitor almost each month. Effective profit strategies are hard to come by in a rapidly changing landscape, which is why I ask you to consider the approach toward Branded Entertainment as a "side business"—one that can promote uniqueness and overall creativity and add more suitable brands to "out-of-the-box" experiences—another way to get revenue in from advertisers seeking change.

MONEY MANAGEMENT

Assembling a new branded deal is a lot like assembling a new production. The new branded deal becomes an independent entity comprised of multiple parties, each party assigning members that will best represent a consolidated unit soon accountable for results. From the perspective of the entity itself, a branded deal will have its own budget and mile markers to hit and be regulated by a cash flow system that will determine when cash is released based on agreed-upon goals.

The party leading the deal usually takes "the plunge" in defining the system and the procedures that will be followed, bearing in mind that a team is being constructed to follow

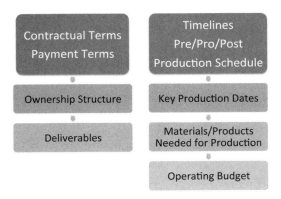

Figure 6.8. Guidelines for a Branded Entertainment deal.

these procedures and that everyone within the team that is making the deal happen needs to know how the process is to flow. One of the things to be accomplished once a team has been formed is to establish guidelines for what will be needed for a deal to happen (and later the guidelines for the people who will assemble it). Each party can then review these guidelines. Establishing the guidelines can be done in the form of a matrix chart (Figure 6.8). The matrix chart is an essential document that addresses money and time. (Creating the matrix chart precedes the creation of a money management system.)

Two guidelines determine the requirements of each party: a timeline and a cash investment. These guidelines are divided into phases: the development/contractual phase, the preproduction phase, and the production/postproduction phase (Figure 6.9). Outline these phases with as much detail as possible: what is needed from the network, the brand, and production. Including detail is essential to ensure that every-

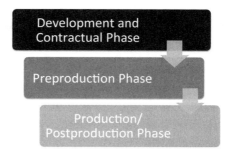

Figure 6.9. Guideline phases.

thing being planned has a corresponding money allocation for execution.

The remainder of this section will focus on:

- How money is planned and budgeted
- How money is contributed/distributed
- How money is allocated

Each of these topics corresponds to one of the three phases.

How Money Is Planned/Budgeted

The planning/budgeting process is performed during the initial phase—development/contractual. In the development/contractual phase, the content idea is still evolving. New details are being added to the idea. All parties are contributing to the development of an overall concept.

Assuming the content idea has now gained enough traction to continue, the next step is to know how much money will be required to bring the content idea to life. This money is attached to the production itself. Production and delivery of the content is considered to be the estimated budget. Additional sections will then be incorporated into the budget as needed. These additional sections could include any extensions to the idea, additional platforms to cover, social media distribution, promotional campaigns, and initial launch efforts—all are part of the initial money requirements to be included in the development/contractual phase. Although specific discussions on profit sharing have probably not occurred, adding some sum of money that more or less corresponds to the amount of revenue to be made by the participating parties is important. A development fee for the producer(s) can also be part of the profit plan.

Important in the development/contractual phase is building in appropriate caveats that will allow for any changes necessary. These numbers certainly tend to change. Although the preliminary numbers are shown to others and regularly presented, all parties must be aware that any additions to the idea or expansion in executing it will have monetary consequences. One way to deal with the possibility of changes in the idea or in its execution is to add a cushion to the production number to deal with arguments about lowering the overall budget number if money is not needed, but typically arguments occur when the budget needs to be raised, even if the reason is to comply with additional requirements of a brand.

How Money Is Contributed/Disbursed

Once the budget planning has been reviewed by all involved parties, it is time to move to the preproduction phase. In this phase, money is reviewed from two angles:

- How contributors divide the overall contribution required for the proposed type of deal according to what they will get in return as an investing party
- How money is disbursed to the production entity responsible for execution

By *contribution*, I mean the percentage each party pays into the overall deal. As mentioned before, not all parties have to contribute to the cash portion of a deal. Traditionally speaking, the brand may very well contribute 100% of the dollars. In more contemporary scenarios, however, networks want to participate in the future of an idea. Hence, networks may be willing to contribute some amount to the overall funding of a Branded Entertainment agreement. Ad agencies also see new business opportunities in developing new content and monetizing it across multiple brands within their roster of clients. At this phase, the budget amounts need to become specific, at least in terms of percentages.

Determining when money is disbursed is essential to making the cash flow of the operation work. During the preproduction of Branded Entertainment content, usually a substantial amount of cash is required upfront. This arrangement, however, is not how brands and networks usually make payments. This difference is the biggest challenge in money management. I recommend breaking down production needs into smaller tasks and "micro analyzing" them. Usually what happens in this process is that by reviewing all of the tasks using a micro approach, identifying which investments need to be made at the start and which ones will allow a 30- or 60-day payment period is easier. If the money required upfront is high, asking one of the investing parties to lend the initial portion may be needed. This party can either serve as a "bank" for the overall deal, with the funds being returned once the project is completed, or the party can later tag this lending portion to their payment which will be billed to the brand. Determining how and when money contributions and disbursements are required should be done in the preproduction phase—before production starts. Doing so will save everyone a lot of production headaches.

As money is disbursed according to the tasks to be accomplished, a weekly report is needed to report the status of task execution. The weekly report indicates the tasks accomplished and the money utilized to make them happen. (Money not used must also be reported.) If money is required that has not been previously budgeted (first upfront to get some tasks going and last as a remainder sum), a request for funds must to be made. A funding request is not part of the weekly report. A funding request is a separate issue that needs to be dealt with in consensus with all parties involved in the deal.

How Money Is Allocated

Money allocation is the last phase of the process and corresponds to production (principal photography) and post-production (editing) assignments of the final deliverable content. Allocation of the final dollars to production is made in this phase. The postdelivery requirements must be finished according to the expectations delineated in the contract. If the initial parties to the deal have requested copies of the product, all copies must also be delivered at this time.

Additional fees considered to be profit are also paid off in this final phase.

The production team can now proceed to collect revenue (known as a *production fee*). I have seen production fee percentages vary over time and over different deals, but the average tends to be in the 10% range.

Other fees can include a *handling fee* for the agency (a commission). The percentages of all these fees are usually part of the overall negotiation between the agency and the brand. These negotiations are done in advance to securing a working budget.

Several parties may have acted as "executive producers" of the content and therefore are able to collect a profit from the production. Executive producers can be from any of the participating parties. Credit for being an executive producer is usually earned by the individuals who were able to contribute to the financial creation of the deal. This fee can be flat or a small percentage of the overall budget. If a development fee was budgeted from the start by one of the parties, this phase is when the fee is paid. The fee awards the work performed at the very start of the process.

If a consultancy fee was attached, this phase is the time to pay it as well. Any of the parties may have included a consultancy fee to oversee the entire process. The range for consultancy fees can be prenegotiated based on the overall budget for production or flat depending on the estimated hours dedicated to the branded deal. (*Note*: I am not a fan of including a consultancy fee based solely on hours. If a deal is concluded early, then there should be a reward for doing so because completing a deal early saves all parties high legal fees.)

There is room for all members of a Branded Entertainment transaction to share in a profit piece for bringing the deal to life. Once the deal has been consummated, it is time to start the process of producing and delivering the content.

In summary, this chapter has detailed the money variable in assembling a Branded Entertainment deal: money as an investment, money as profit to a business, and management of money as it is allocated to the deal according to the provisions of the deal. Demonstrating that agencies, media platforms, and independents can come to the table and successfully create a new way to do business with a brand is becoming easier and easier. For the brand, the format for a deal is more innovative, allowing the brand to be included and to have an ability to implement a market strategy that has the brand at the epicenter of each unfolding episode.

Cash infusion. In money transactions, the first execution related to money is cash infusion. An idea that eventually generates a Branded Entertainment deal requires cash upfront as an investment for development and execution. Obtaining upfront money requires inviting brands, media outlets, and producers for consideration as participants. Through a process of selection and review, one or more parties may be able and willing to advance the cash needed to get the deal in motion. The investment itself is basically for the creative work that assembles a great idea for consumers, with the attributes of a brand intertwined within the content and a plan for release to the masses by a particular media platform. The investment corresponds to a partial or full expenditure needed to take an idea from its initial stage to the final stage when the idea becomes content ready to be aired.

Profit. The second execution related to money transactions is having an understanding of how these new deals will be transformed into a successful business model. By *successful*, the implication is that each one of the parties that comes to the table will make money considered to be profit. The initial investment generates a return. In business, common terminology for this profit is return on investment. All participating parties, even the ones who are considered as only work for hire, expect to make a profit by coming together on a deal of this nature. This aspect of Branded Entertainment deals is known as "profit imperatives" because it serves as a magnet for new players. Once Branded Entertainment deals reveal their success in money terms, more media outlets, brands, and agencies are piqued with interest to include Branded Entertainment deals on their future business radar.

Money management. The third and last execution related to money is money management. Obtaining money is easy compared to managing it. During money management, a team of Branded Entertainment experts works diligently for all parties, strategizing how money is planned and budgeted, how it is distributed or disbursed, and how it is allocated to the execution of the idea. This strategizing is reasonably harder because the decisions behind each one of these areas is usually not unilateral. The decisions require opinions and approvals on a regular basis. The key to success is to stay true to the timelines. Be sure to implement a realistic delineation of the time it takes to move from phase to phase. If the timelines are created well in advance, and reviewed and honored by all parties, then the money management process has a chance to be a contributor to the deal as opposed to being a burden.

CHAPTER 7

Mechanics and Metrics

I equate getting a handle on Branded Entertainment to something most of us can relate to: learning a new dance. Watching or judging from the outside is easy enough, but once the actual learning process starts, certain things need to flow smoothly for dancing to look and feel effortless. The flow of a dance is only captured after each one of the steps has been learned and rehearsed. So, now that the steps, the parties involved, and the elements of a branded deal have been reviewed one by one, it is time for the "full dance" of the deal to unfold and for us to be equipped with the appropriate tools for appraising the final performance.

DEAL MECHANICS AND FLOW

Let's review what has been covered thus far and start to build the overall flow of a deal. Up to now, there has been a description of each step necessary to put a deal in motion. There has been disclosure of who is involved and the roles of each player. There has been a detailed list of the elements needed to consider the deal "doable."

The Idea

What type of idea triggers a Branded Entertainment deal? Is it an idea that fulfills a content need in the marketplace? Is the idea born out of a brand's request for a particular target demographic? Is an agency creating an idea in an effort to own the content and present it to several clients?

How the initial idea comes to life is important. The initiator is the starting point for determining who will lead the deal in the near future. As discussed in Chapter 5, there are no limitations as to which party generates the idea. Just because a brand makes a request does not automatically mean the brand is willing to lead the deal. The deal may be ultimately led by the brand's agency or even by an independent production company. On the other hand, just because a brand does not generate the initial idea does not mean that the brand cannot lead the deal that follows. In essence, having the seed to an idea carries an inherent advantage, but having this seed does not pass on the right to the leading role during the entire process. The true weight for who eventually leads the deal has more to do with the party who truly understands how to put the deal together. Ideas are great to have, but those who actually transform them into a deal can raise the level of the entire experience for everyone involved.

The Pitch

The idea is then turned into a pitch. The pitch basically brings the idea to life with the brand in mind so others can envision how far this idea can go and how creatively the brand can be intertwined into engaging content. At the pitch stage, other potential participants can be invited to watch the initial process move forward. For example, if the pitch is being given to a brand by an independent producer, the agency of that brand or a media outlet can be invited to sit in. Having a "home" (a media outlet) where the content can live also adds strength to the pitch process. Having a media outlet basically indicates that the idea is ready to be launched if the brand agrees with the direction of the pitch.

The most likely scenario, with the pitch initially starting with the brand for several reviews, includes:

- If the brand likes the idea but has no media outlet selected at this point, the same pitch will be given to several media options. Having the brand already behind the idea makes a big difference when moving through the process—it allows the possibility of shopping the idea around. Then a decision can be made about which media outlet is best suited for a partnership.
- If the network/media outlet is the party pitching the brand, then the next step is to pitch the idea to a list of production partners and select the one that best interprets the idea with the right budget in mind.

The Team and the Proposal

By now, the parties for the deal have been preselected. I say "pre" because once the proposal is on the table for presentation, there is always a chance that one of the preselected parties will choose not to continue (one of the reasons why the Branded Entertainment process is not black and white). At this stage, when matters of budget and ownership can be touched upon, some parties may agree on any or all of the components of a Branded Entertainment deal and some may simply walk away.

The proposal is assembled early on by team members who have a solid understanding of the idea and know where it can be taken to get to a final YES. This early assembled team is in control of generating an initial budget, which will give all parties an idea of what is required as an initial investment. This is the time to contemplate disclosure of the initial budget, if more than one investing party might be needed. For example, a brand at this point might disclose the working budget it has for a project. If the amount in the budget is short of the total needed to fully execute the project, finding a network/media outlet with the capacity to invest may be a solution. This is the crossroads where a potential network could say YES and the proposal for the deal keeps moving forward, or the network might choose to walk away—and the search continues.

Note: The branded team assembled to close a deal should be a blend of people with content development experience and brand "know-how," meaning a true understanding of the brand's procedures, objectives, and funding sources within. The ideal team needs to be made up of only key people. Less is better in this case to function effectively and quickly react in case a potential partner drops out and a new one needs to be located. This team must possess the innate ability to listen carefully to all sides and extract the essence of what each side needs and expects. This is the time when the proposal will likely go through some mutations and evolve into something all parties can finally agree to.

As time goes by and the deal keeps evolving, some final decision makers tend to imagine what the idea will look like and forget the parameters previously discussed at the starting point. The success of the branded team lies in bringing all parties to a "reality check" periodically throughout the entire process. This practice will save a lot of time at the end, and time, as we all know, means money.

The Right Agreements and Paperwork

At the point when the final proposal has been reviewed and approved by the interested parties, it is time to decide how the agreements are to be structured. As I mentioned earlier, there is no need to follow the course of a one-size-fits-all mentality. For example, the way in which an agency works with a brand is sometimes very private, so there may still be a need to continue to structure the agreement separately. Depending on which party leads the overall agreement, a network may choose to produce the content in-house or hire a production entity and create an agreement solely with them. That same network may then turn around and build an agreement directly with the agency or the brand. The important part of this process is to make sure all parties are "tied up" in terms of responsibilities, accountability, and deliverables.

The next step is to generate attachments to the agreements. Create charts and systems to organize the timeline, cash flows, and duties of each party. The final approved working budget is also part of the paperwork necessary to move forward.

The basic rule of paperwork is to make sure all parties are bound, committed, and clear on their deliverables. These deliverables are the expected product, completed at the right time, and either on or under budget.

Leadership

By the time this part of the process is reached, which one of the participating parties is the natural leader for the process is usually clear. Remember, leadership can come from any of the parties (the agency, the network, a production company, or the brand itself). Leadership may also be directly related to the party who brought the initial idea to the table.

Now it is time to make some determinations about selecting the decisive companies that will come into the deal as participants of the branded team. There is no formula set in stone as to who these members should be. The qualifier for team members is to ensure that each member has a particular skill needed to assemble a deal efficiently (e.g., creative development, brand know-how, media expertise, etc.). I highly recommend making the team small—ideally no more than three to four participants.

One team member is the leader of the deal. The leader ensures all information flows accordingly to the rest of the people involved from each party. The leader also holds the rest of the team members accountable for getting replies and evaluations from the parties to the deal in accordance with the subsequent moves that will lead to the production execution.

Cash Infusion and Profit Imperatives

The final touch to assembling the production of a branded deal is to set the right dollar amount for the budget. Is the overall funding being provided by one party or more? How will the funding be divided and when will it be allocated? Is there any revenue to be made afterward? Is there an opportunity to create a subsequent opportunity to monetize the branded content once this first deal is completed? This is the time to create the final budget. The final budget should include the investment required from each party involved in the deal.

This is also the time to define what constitutes profit for the parties working throughout the execution of the content. In the budget being set, profit can be categorized as production fees, as line item roles in the budget (above the line), or as development fees. Future monetization such as a syndication deal, a format sale, or other venues for airing the content can also be added to the final cash/profit layout. These incremental revenues can be represented in percentages of the budget because these revenues may still be considered as potential and not actual. Clarity on money matters allows everyone to understand what it will take to get the project off the ground. Next, it is time to create reporting systems to handle cash management.

Money Management

The system to be created will always be unique to each deal. Each Branded Entertainment deal has different parties and different interests that add different variables, making no two deals the same. The first key aspect regarding money management is knowing exactly when and where the money will be spent. The second key aspect is to ensure the cash flow is in line with production timelines. If cash comes from more than one source, it is crucial to know exactly what the funding schedule of each investing party will be. It is one thing to agree on paper to make an investment and another to know when that money will actually be injected into the production account.

The funding schedule is something that needs to be taken into consideration when building a production schedule. Be aware that an invoice sent is not an invoice paid! Brands are known for having their own internal rules for payment. Learning about these internal rules before the deal is in progress is advisable. Billing cycles can sometimes exceed 120 days.

As a safety measure, make one of the contracting parties the "bank" for all the required funding. As the process evolves and the deliverables are completed, funding that comes in will then be fully paid to this party. A small percentage fee can be added to the overall agreement for the party serving the branded deal as the bank of the overall transaction.

Creating a system/schedule for the product delivery needed for the production is vital. This task falls in the lap of the brand. Following a timely schedule to stay on course with the established timeline is imperative. A delay in the product(s) being featured by the brand (the actual item that will be blended within the content) can cause overages on the entire production. Determine in advance how overages and underages will be handled in the production budget.

MEASUREMENT AND METRICS

How to create value in the branded business and how to measure results are two reasons why Branded Entertainment deals are still not typical for the masses. These deals tend to be more "boutique" than "retail" style. They are created for a few brands rather than for all brands. Historically, brands have always looked for a quantitative measure to gather results. The results can prove if the effectiveness of the executed idea of content with a brand inside was significant enough to recoup the investment or meet a greater goal. The results help brands decide what to do next. Nontraditional strategies on how to impact consumers may not necessarily offer a quantitative measuring system to easily arrive at a conclusive determination of success. There are, however, parameters that can be used to measure results. In Branded Entertainment deals created from scratch, success should not only be measured by ratings or impressions but also by qualitative factors that provide a better understanding of how the target audience received the message. Branded deals do not tend to follow quantitative measures only. Traditional media measurements do matter, but they are not the only way to confirm success. It is important to think beyond simple ratings or households delivered.

An initial list of parameters can be considered (Figure 7.1). These parameters offer ways to measure success in a more expanded scenario. The list can be adapted depending on the brand's goals and preferences. Later, these metrics will be of use in future case studies during new pitches and proposals:

- Brand integration and endemic presence
- Brand awareness and engagement
- Lead generation and acquisition
- Sales metrics and traffic generation

Figure 7.1. Parameters to consider for measuring the success of a branded deal.

Brand Integration and Endemic Presence

When goals are set and a brand chooses a particular marketing strategy specifically related to branded content, a prevailing question arises: "How do we measure performance?" Now, knowing beforehand whether the brand is seeking "awareness" or looking for immediate "action" from the consumer is important. Be clear on this from the start. Knowing what a brand strategy seeks in advance can guide the Branded Entertainment team to better define a creative mission for the content about to be conceived (Figure 7.2). This knowledge will set the parameters for a brand's presence within the content—what is known as brand integration.

Endemic presence is a term now being widely used by brands and agencies. Endemic presence implies that the presence of a brand must blend right in with the content in a natural way that is not forced. In fact, in endemic presence

Immediate Action From Consumers?

Brand Awareness By Customers?

BRAND INTEGRATION STRATEGY

Figure 7.2. Does the brand want immediate action from consumers or brand awareness by consumers?

Blend In a Natural Way, Not Forced

Blend With Content to Create an Emotional Connection

ENDEMIC PRESENCE

Figure 7.3. Endemic presence: the presence of the brand blends into the content, the script or the central plot, naturally.

the brand is woven in like another character within the content itself. A brand's attributes are brought to life "softly," but they are firmly intertwined into the script itself or the plot of the central theme (Figure 7.3).

A brand is endemically present when it "bleeds" into content appropriately. The tone of the message should inspire some action from the consumer or it should create an emotional connection or set an aspiration into motion.

Measuring the value of this type of integration, known as *active integration*, is possible. Active integrations can be measured in seconds within the content and their value can be at least three times the value of a traditional message. By traditional, I am comparing an active integration to the value of a standard 30-second commercial. If the brand-in-content is truly endemic, the impact should be high and have little if any rejection from the viewer. Viewers are witnessing the brand as a true character of the content—this result is what the brands are after.

Brand Awareness and Engagement

Measuring the impact a brand can have within content is performed through what is known as *passive integration*. In passive integration, the brand has a place within the plot, but the brand is not enhanced or emphasized as much as a character. The brand is present but not actively engaged. The brand-in-content is present to show a character's loyalty to a particular brand. Passive integrations are also measured in seconds, like active integrations, but passive integrations have a lesser value—anywhere from one to two times a traditional advertising second (Figure 7.4).

Another area that can be measured is the channel delivery process. A multi-channel delivery strategy means that the brand-in-content travels to consumers through multiple touch points (points where a brand "touches" the consumer). Touch points are multiple media outlets such as TV, cable, radio, mobisodes (condensed series episodes distributed to cellular phones), webisodes (series episodes distributed as web television), events, "behind the scenes," and social

Active Integrations

• 3X Value of Traditional 30-Second Spot*

Passive Integrations

• 1X or 2X Value of Traditional 30-Second Spot*

Figure 7.4. A valuation model for active and passive integrations. Passive integrations have lesser value than active integrations. * The time period scheduled for airing the branded content determines the variation of value of the 30 seconds used to create the valuation of integrations.

media, to mention a few (Figure 7.5). By delivering to more than one platform, a brand can measure reactivity, viewing patterns, and general "likeness" from the ultimate consumer. Consumer touch points are an area in which results are gathered and tallied. (The assumption here is that goals have been delineated from the start of the deal.)

Lead Generation and Acquisition

Consumer engagement also leads a brand to explore extensions to measure the recently created content. These extensions invite consumers to take action. Taking action can be in the form of promotions, sweepstakes, and short-term offers or participating in fun games and events in which consumers

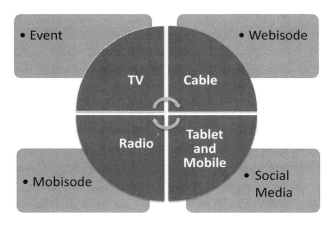

Figure 7.5. A multi-channel/platform delivery strategy for brand-in-content traveling to consumers via multiple touch points.

actively intend to win something or try something engaging that has entertainment value for them, e.g., entering a contest in which the winner gets to attend a tailgate party prior to a sporting event, a VIP party prior to a concert, or an award show.

Brands can conduct their own proprietary research to measure awareness levels on a more individual basis. Alternately, the research can be done by a third party who gathers the information and then sells it to the brand. The goal is to acquire relevant engagement information about the brand and its impact on the consumer. This tool can be used as a "filter" to help weed out consumers who are not inter-ested and to lead the brand to customers who might engage with the brand more favorably.

Sales Metrics and Traffic Generation

Sales metrics and traffic generation are commonly used in the industry and they are not strangers to brand managers. Sales metrics and traffic generation are considered to be good measuring bars of success.

Sales metrics. The key point to remember when gathering sales metrics is to assess and clearly define from the beginning of a branded deal where the starting and end points are when sales are to be measured. Whether the measurement is done in the form of dollars, cases, or items sold, the key thing here is to measure sales during a time when no other significant marketing activity is being conducted. If the marketing of the branded deal is not conducted nationwide, then reflecting this situation in the comparison, so the numbers are legitimate, is important. Be sure to include useful figures on future case studies. These numbers can have a big impact in making future decisions about bigger endeavors in Branded Entertainment.

Traffic generation. Measuring traffic generation can take place at a retail level. Marketing efforts directly linked to potential consumers can be designed ahead of time as the Branded Entertainment deal is being engineered. I recall a very successful example when a brand (a car company) linked the sale of an actual TV series to the sales of a new vehicle. Dealers would talk about the new traffic that emerged during the time when the series aired on TV. Potential customers would walk into the car company's dealerships asking for the complete series package which was being promoted at the end of each episode.

If a brand does not have a retail outlet for sales, then traffic generation can be determined on multi-level platforms in which content-related activities can be carefully placed, assuming they have been designed in advance during concept development. Content-related activities include, but are not limited to:

- Social media platform activities in which new relationships are made with potential new consumers
- An official website for the newly created branded content with various incentives such as winning a prize
- Consumers competing against each other by making something of creative value to get a prize of some relevance
- Playing a clever game that gets consumers hooked through a series of new elevated challenges

These traffic measures generate leads as long as a process is developed to quantify details about who the consumer is.

The most important thing to remember is that branded deals are not only qualitative, but they can be quantified in more ways than ratings only. This nature of branded deals can "incentivize" a brand to continue being creative regarding how consumer impact can be measured and interpreted. Most empowering seems to be that even the quantification process can be part of the creative development process—a brand can create new ways to measure behavior by consumers. Brands love content creation, but they also realize the importance of designing metrics to best understand how these efforts measure up in the end. Many brand leaders understand that statistics for measuring and interpreting success can also be created and conceived from scratch. I

Content
Out-of-the Box Financial Models
Measurement Metrics

Creativity at All Levels

Figure 7.6. A branded deal has creativity at many levels: content, financial models, and measurement metrics for customer behavior and success.

encourage new brand clients to come up with new and additional ways to measure results. After all, creativity is what Branded Entertainment deals represent—creativity at all levels (Figure 7.6).

CHAPTER 8

Case Study

A scripted series takes brands to a protagonist role ...

An article published in *The New York Times* on October 28, 2011, entitled *Script Takes Sponsors from Bit Players to a Starring Role*, by Stuart Elliott, summarized the epic process of marrying brands to a new scripted series on a known network. In this scripted series, the Branded Entertainment was well defined, but product placement differed from similar deals. According to Elliott, "The practice, known as Branded Entertainment or branded integration, is more extensive than so-called product placement because a brand buying its way into a show gets a prominent role rather than a bit part. Advertisers and agencies like Branded Entertainment because it counters the ability of viewers to avoid commercials; if they try skipping the branded portions of the show, they could miss salient plot points."[1]

---

[1]Stuart Elliott, "Script Takes Sponsors from Bit Players to a Starring Role," *The New York Times*, October 27, 2011 (available at NYT.com) and October 28, 2011, p. B4.

Elliott's article was dedicated in its entirety to one of the shows produced by Animus Entertainment Group, the company founded by the author 11 years ago. The article defined who the participating brands were and gave examples of how these brands were brought to life. The brands included a global airline, a fast food company, an American car company, a domestic beer group, and a home improvement company. Having five brands in a scripted series made the product placement process into a story worth telling and worthy of sharing.

THE IDEA AND THE NEW CONTENT

In this Branded Entertainment deal, a content developer (independent producer) led the deal. In this particular scenario, the need the producers intended to fill was a void of scripted content that the network had encountered for some years. Beginning from the time when the Branded Entertainment idea came about to fill a need to its conclusion, the TV deal required 12 months. (*Note*: To retain anonymity, the names of the network, brands, and people will not be used in this case study.)

The new content started as an idea for a TV series. The idea was ignited by a group of independent producers who needed help in carrying a deal forward. After I met the group of independent producers, I realized the idea had potential to evolve into a pitch, but the group was unable to do the development alone. So we made an agreement to be 50/50 partners. The group of independent producers would bring the idea to the partnership and Animus would carry out the rest. Animus would also be responsible for overseeing the entire deal if it came to fruition.

The only way to know if the idea had true potential was to present it to the first player: an agency. By making the first presentation to the agency, we as producers (the content developers from Animus) were able to meet with the brand managers and present the pitch. A small team was formed to carry out making the pitch to the brand. The team was comprised of a creative executive from the independent production company, an agency leader who understood media, and me. I participated in the role of determining what a brand might want—I was the decipherer.

The material developed into the pitch had multiple components:

1. A formal presentation of the idea and the potential participation of more than one brand
2. A mini-video or mini-pilot created by the Animus partners, who had generated the idea in the first place, that showcased the overall idea for the series and starred the principal talent

The video was less than 10 minutes long. It slowly revealed the content idea with a few phrases and featured video shots of the main cast revealing important climatic points of the story and B-rolls that were to mimic a compilation of episodes from the series. With the help of generic images of soccer being played that were coupled with clips showing the fury of the sports fans in reaction, the video successfully kept the audience (the network in this case) at several meetings wanting to know more about the plot.

The agency leader became quite engaged in the process and subsequently became more and more involved in developing the pitch for a brand. Something interesting happened at this point. The agency leader realized that the idea needed to be taken to more than one brand. Her preference was to go after other brands that were part of the agency's roster—made sense. Later on, when the idea caught the attention of several brands, we as producers reserved our rights to go after some independent brands that were not affiliated with the agency. Because our ability to approach nonaffiliated independent brands had been made clear from the start, the agency leader gave us the go ahead.

THE FIRST BRAND

The first brand we met with was an American car company. The meeting had the right mix of decision makers, interesting questions, and a desire to know what the next steps would be. The agency leader and the car company brand managers needed clarification on one key point before sealing a deal: confirmation of the network that would air the content.

At this point, the next step in the process was to decide which networks were viable candidates for the series. In an effort to be efficient, the list of candidates considered only a few players. Meetings with the networks were arranged and, as expected, the first rounds were with bigger broadcasters.

The three team members who initiated this process attended the meetings with broadcasters. I as the independent producers' representative was a member. The other two members were the agency leader and the brand manager who had asked for confirmation of the network that would air the content. This initial branded team needed to demonstrate an advance commitment for the deal—a deal comprised of multiple parties in which two were already teamed up with us, the producers in the initial phase. A third party still needed to be secured—a network. Each team member would be an integral part of the next task we all had to embark on.

The first two network meetings were discouraging. The bottom line for both media outlets was their participation in exchange for a heavy dose of cash from the brands. The media outlets wanted the series to be fully funded by the brands plus an amount of media support by each brand that exceeded the average annual increase of the brands' current annual spending. Additionally, both networks asked for an enormous timeline for presenting the idea internally.

WHEN IT WAS TIME TO REGROUP

At this point in the process, because of the lengthy time demands of the first two networks, we needed to reconsider our options. (*Note*: Usually when a network is given a certain amount of time to respond, the idea is not to be shown to any other network, which results in dead time when there is no assurance that a deal will actually happen with the network.) Fortunately, another network was interested—"smaller" in terms of eyeball coverage but more targeted to a sports audience. Our concern, however, was that our research had shown that this smaller network was not big on scripted content. This concern was not enough to stop us—it was our last best option.

The other network had walked away from scripted content after a previous series experience went "sour" for them some 7 years ago. Since then, no one had presented the right idea with the appropriate thematic appeal that would ring a bell for the network's new decision makers. This network, however, had something the others did not: a strong desire to make a difference with something unique. The network also had a person who was not afraid to lead from within. (*Note*: The two networks already pitched with this idea were not eager to create change within their established ranks and procedures.)

Looking back, the key to making this deal happen was in deciding to whom the idea should be presented *inside* the network. As content producers, we could have simply taken the idea to people inside the programming department at the network. We also knew some ad sales people, but they would have had a hard time being the type of change agents that we needed within the network to make this deal happen to get the content on the air. Our agency leader, however, knew someone high up at the network. So she called this contact and asked for advice as to whom this type of proposal should be taken. The answer came back: take the pitch to the person in charge of content business development. Finding a decision maker at the content business development level who has the ability to champion a project within a network is uncommon. The key here, however, was that the person in charge of content business development became very invested in the project after seeing the preview reel and listening to our ideas. The pitch made an enormous difference, and the support of the brand and the agency was invaluable, but what everyone had hoped and prayed for happened—we had an insider, a champion who was not afraid to take, and sell, our idea to his superiors. (He could also gain a lot career-wise if the project were green-lit.)

At the end of the first meeting, I vividly remember the content business development manager's last words as he walked us out: "I need you all to understand that we as a network are very big and *big* means *slow* ... but I believe this [idea] has the potential to change the course of our decision of shying away from scripted content. To me, this content is the right way to get back in. Have patience. I promise to keep you in the loop every step of the way." Funny how those words did not mean "yes," but they were enough to keep us from knocking on more doors. (One advantage of being on a team is the ability to check in with each other to be sure we are all on the same page. In this instance, we all had the same reaction.)

WHILE WE WAITED

We had a few things to accomplish while waiting for a decision from the network.

The automotive brand. First, we reignited our conversations with the automotive brand and began selling the benefits of going with a smaller network. Our summary was that by doing so the smaller network would provide greater flexibility for the automotive brand and bring to the table a true partner who would enter the project with new ideas. Last, but certainly not least, the smaller network was not afraid to co-fund the idea with cash. As our conversations continued, the network agreed to spearhead the content agreement. Because the network was a cash partner as well, they would control the flow of cash to the production.

Noncompeting brands within the agency. Second, we went after other noncompeting brands. Some of these brands were part of the agency (later on, some of the brands were not). The fact that we had received a "soft yes" from the car company (they were waiting for confirmation of the network that would air the content) meant that other brands could trust this newly legitimized process. The car company would be the headliner of our show; now all we needed was to book the opening acts. As a result, the series of meetings conducted with the other brand leaders were more geared toward the creative area. For instance, for a fast food company we demonstrated how one of their products would become an icon for practicing sports and for feeding the insatiable hunger after a game.

Brands outside the agency. Third, brands outside the agency's roster of clients were now curious enough to listen to our innovative approach to content and brands within a series. We took the time to present the TV series intertwined with ways to weave in their brand. We met with a home improvement company that had participated in previous Branded Entertainment ventures ignited by us. The rapport was excellent. So we took the idea directly to the brand without the agency leader but with the understanding that as the lead agency, the agency would have two to three slots reserved within the show (not a concern for us or the brand). The home improvement brand manager was immediately interested and wanted to meet with the agency of record (which sometimes can equate to being the leading agency for a business such as this). The agency of record was known for being progressive and believed in the power of Branded Entertainment deals—clearly a favorable situation. We, as producers, had never worked with this agency so we put our best foot forward. Multiple brand integration ideas were asked for from us by this agency; these ideas were for other brands the agency had in their client roster. These requests were all carefully evaluated. After the meeting with the agency, the brand manager from the home improvement company checked in with us and insisted on being a part of a dramatic moment within the plot of the story. (When a brand leader is so clear on what seems important to them, the request deserves true consideration.)

Meanwhile, conversations with the smaller network were coming together. We received feedback within 6 weeks of our first meeting that the idea had been well received by ad sales and programming. Then, the network asked us to submit a production budget for review. Once reviewed, the next question by the network was: "How much of this budget can be funded by the brands?" (*Note*: This is a tough, but necessary, question to answer. No matter how many proposals are out there pending with brands, no real numbers are inked because there is not yet a network commitment. This is one of the toughest hurdles to overcome.)

So the next step was to budget how much the brands could fund, assuming a viewership level based on an estimated time period by the channel for this particular show. Once viewership was estimated/established, the network would determine if they were able to provide the deficit funding needed to assume the production budget.

Once the production budget was submitted, a different process would continue inside the network. The network had to green-light the content and assume the remainder of the investment. (*Note*: The new content idea was considered by the network to be a big plus to be unveiled at the "upfront" presentation held annually for advertisers each May.)

From a cash perspective, the combined contribution of all of the brands would add up to about 60% of the total production budget, meaning the network needed to provide the remaining 40%. The network commitment came with conditions. The network wanted the 40% to be reduced and instructed the ad sales team from the network to work toward an increase on ad spending from the brands. Our task was to meet with them, evaluate the current investment from the brands, and team up to add brand ideas that would secure additional media dollars for the network.

WHEN THE TRUE BRANDED ENTERTAINMENT PROCESS BEGAN

With a conditional green-light, it was time for us to go back to the drawing board and secure some creative ways to enlarge the "idea basket" for each brand's total participation in and around the content. The creative leader from our team and I (acting as the brand decoder) met to develop multiple ways to stretch the reach of the brands beyond the TV show. These ideas included surrounding the series with digital content—additional content that would be created by a viewer based on a contest in which the winner and the star of the series would attend a VIP premiere event. The contest was supported by public relations dissemination to actual sports fans. These fans were the hard-core audience of the channel—viewers whose primary entertainment consumption was sports content.

Once the brands received proposals from the network to increase their spending, the negotiations began and an additional 20% was raised. Now, with 80% funding by the brands, we were ready to move to the contract stage. Because so much money was coming from the brands and because of their added investment in the network, the decision was made at this point to have the network lead the contract negotiations.

THE CONTRACTUAL PROCESS

The brands also needed to agree to make the deal with the network. For the deal to be approved, certain caveats had to be put into place. The network had to agree that we as the producers had the creative green-light to execute the content we had previously agreed upon with the brands (that were now jumping on board with us at the time of the deal). Later on, once the deal had been defined with the network, when new brands joined, the creative decisions on content to be generated for these new comers would go though a new process: first with the network; later we as producers would refine the ideas as the creative team within the deal. The network would then have final approval. This arrangement meant we would be the originators of the ideas for the brands inside the script. The money negotiated with the brands for the Branded Entertainment portions went directly to the ad sales "bucket." The programming department made an internal agreement to add the difference in necessary funding to the production deal.

We and the network, as creators, then needed to negotiate the rights and ownership. (This agreement still remains confidential.) We had a deal with the network to produce and deliver the series as the budget stated. Additionally, we had creative responsibility for the brands. The deals with each brand would be handled directly by the network. In summary, we created one agreement between the producers and the network, and the network secured agreements with each brand with two components: the Branded Entertainment part and the ad sales support of the series. The brands had to adhere to the same payment structure the network had for clients. The network had to agree to a cash flow payment plan that would not jeopardize the timeline for this multimillion-dollar production.

A TRUE WIN-WIN

The creators and producers benefitted from a traditional production fee plus a content creation fee that was tagged onto the production budget. The participating agencies had a different agreement with the brands. One agency did so for the sake of making a name in the Branded Entertainment world. The other agency added the overall spending of this deal to their overall commission. The network received new incremental dollars from existing clients in addition to securing a new brand for their roster. On the programming side, the network was able to commission an entire new series for 20% of the production cost. (On a more personal level, the champion of this deal within the network received a promotion to the big brother network with added responsibilities linked to content creation.)

Getting in at the beginning of the Branded Entertainment process was the key for all of the participating brands. From we as producers coming to the table to the network's negotiation with brands secured to co-finance the deal, the brands had a chance to jump-start the creative process within unique content. Each brand was exposed to writers who considered the brand to be a character. Each brand also had a chance to review the thematic plot and to be woven into pivotal moments—moments that would eventually have a stake in future seasons of the series. Even though the actual deal would eventually be inked with the network directly, each brand that walked into this deal early was secured participation unlike any traditional ad sales idea. This for a brand was the true way into creation.

After all was said and done, *The New York Times* article could not have said it better. A brand could be a pillar in the plot of a TV series. Each brand had a role to play alongside characters who became fan favorites. Ultimately, being *seen* is not the same as being engaged with consumer emotions. In an age of detached hyper-selective viewing, those who understand how to emotionally engage their target audience will hold the keys to both today's innovation and tomorrow's standard operating procedures.

CHAPTER 9

Building In Guidelines as a Document

This chapter contains a sample document, known as a *term sheet*, outlining some basic guidelines for starting the process of a potential Branded Entertainment deal between the initiating parties. In the scenario used in this sample document, an agency has piqued the interest of a brand from their client roster and opened the door to the possibility of the brand investing in branded content. In this document, the advertising agency leads the process with a production company. Because the brand responded positively, the agency now has a meeting with a production company to brief them, suggesting an outline for a starting process.

A request for proposal (RFP) or related documentation has been submitted to the production company (Prod Co in document) along with all requirements and ideas about how the project is being envisioned by the agency and the brand client. Once the briefing process and the RFP are submitted to the production company, a document in the form of a term sheet is generated in response to the agency's directive. This document can then be circulated to multiple production companies prior to the selection of the one that will work best for the brand's objectives.

The big differentiating point among the production companies during the selection process is to find a producer who understands how the brand is to be woven into the content versus a producer who will just make content. *Note*: In the Branded Entertainment selection process, when a good production company is found, this entity will most likely receive repeat business. Presently, no abundance of companies that have been granted this type of work, and have done it well, exists. This guidelines document will help grow the business from all angles, including the independents, thus giving rise to more Branded Entertainment deals.

TERMS AND CONDITIONS
TERM SHEET EXAMPLE
Agency and Production Company

STAGE I: CONCEPT DEVELOPMENT AND PRESENTATION
a. Agency Disclosures

Agency discloses that content development can take place, but no guarantees are made that the costs will be covered unless a deal is signed. To avoid unnecessary misunderstandings, being upfront with this element is required. Production Company (Prod Co) has the option to stay. Prod Co should have a cost in mind to produce the content that is included in the budget. This cost assumes everything works out. Prod Co should be willing to walk away if the numbers will not work.

b. Communications Process

Brand and Agency are to add Prod Co to all content-related communication. (As basic as this statement may seem, sometimes getting all the right people connected to the initial process takes a while. Including the production company in all content-related communications from the start ensures effective communications.) Prod Co will then assign the appropriate point person(s) to address each request.

Note: Agency divisions such as the media and the account management departments are aligned, or on the same page, in the action steps that follow.

c. Initial Story Development

The initial story development process breaks down into:

Developing the Concept

Estimate realistic timing. Depending on the length of the series or the type of production, the process of developing the idea could take one or several weeks from conception to creating a short treatment. For scripted shows to have a solid idea built into a fleshed-out treatment, developing the idea could take up to a month. To maximize the effective use of the Prod Co's initial development process, the ideation process needs sufficient information from the Agency regarding client goals on content, including vision, do's and don'ts, and expectations. Sample requests include:

- A minimum of 7 to 10 business days is required for delivery of a concept.
- Prod Co initiates brainstorming meetings and involves top key Agency executives in the process as the ideation process evolves.
- Prod Co requests being present when the idea is taken to the Brand to ensure clarity on what can and cannot be delivered.

Establishing Clear Goals

If budget parameters are included in the RFP, then staying within the budget suggested by the Brand's agency is clearly ideal. Within those guidelines, the goal is to outline in the treatment what can be done and, if needed, what cannot be accomplished. In other words, focus on potential and restrictions (but focus more on potential than restrictions!). Establishing parameters and guidelines that are realistic for the Prod Co's developed concept is one way to make the Brand feel more at ease and truly pay attention to the creative part of the development process.

Creating an Initial Branded Team

Formation of the initial branded team occurs in the earliest stages of developing a small team that can focus on the vision of how the presentation to the media outlet will take place. Members of the team could include the Agency (one representative from account management), one representative from the media, and a creative executive and a top executive from the Prod Co who leads the team.

d. Budgets and the Contract Approval Process

Once there is agreement on the creative concept to be developed, the initial branded team can move toward budgeting:

- A realistic "ballpark" figure is given by the Agency to assemble a budget. Prod Co has the right to review and adjust the budget up to three times (with the purpose of accommodating all requests).

- Subject to senior management availability, a minimum of 10 business days is needed to submit a working budget (version 1).
- Assumptions made will be attached to the budget to clarify what is included in the quote provided.
- Delivery of merchandise and materials from the Brand to Prod Co will impact overall deliverables and the timeline. This factor must be taken into consideration when assembling the final budget with corresponding revisions.
- Itemize anything that *may not be* automatically included in the production budget, e.g.,
    - Merchandise/materials purchases: Development/production costs of content do not include any of the client's merchandise/materials/products being featured within a show or series, short or long form.
    - Agency team travel: Client and Agency travel is to be addressed. If travel is not included in the production budget, instruct Prod Co to include travel expenses before the overall budget is finalized.

e. Contracts

All contracts will be issued and signed *before* any preproduction begins. Contract signatures are due within a week (unless specified) and agreed upon in advance of a different timeline by both parties.

f. Payment Schedule

Payment due dates are to be honored to preserve production timetables and deadlines, e.g.:

- Allocate at least 30% of the production budget to kick off preproduction.
- All other payments between Agency and Prod Co are to be outlined in the contract with a final payment due upon complete delivery of all material.

Note: As a general rule, state that no preproduction work can take place until the contract is signed and the first payment is received by Prod Co.

g. Timing for Review

The media outlet will have a meaningful right of consultation *prior to* preproduction:

- It is absolutely necessary that all parties involved agree on day-to-day execution and sign off on the timetable for deliverables on commissioned content.
- If delays on approvals are encountered during the production timetable, Prod Co can revise deliverables to accommodate any time adjustments which will affect the original timetable (must be approved by the Agency on behalf of the Brand).
- All changes agreed upon post-timeline may impact the overall budget and delivery dates.

STAGE II: PREPRODUCTION

a. Casting

Specify the amount of time needed to perform scouting and casting, e.g., 30 to 90 days will be required for scouting and casting (depends on the project; it can be more time).

Recommendations and Deadlines for Final Casting Selections:

- Prod Co will supply a maximum of three options for:
  - Participants
  - Host(s)
  - Any other casting required
- Client must arrive at a final selection within 2 weeks of receiving viable options (as an average).
- Delays on finalizing the selection process may have an impact on the timetable and budget.

b. Master Plan Meeting

Schedule a meeting concerning having one common production location. This meeting is to include all parties (Agency, Brand, and Prod Co). Another purpose of this meeting is to review the master plan:

- Meeting is headed by a member of the Branded Entertainment team. Meeting determines any final changes needing to be approved.

- Once all parties agree to all new specs, the Branded Entertainment team will design an outline for project execution.
- Any additional changes or requests will delay the delivery schedule and impact the approved budget.

c. Merchandise/Materials Coordination

- The Agency may lead the effort in coordinating the itemization, access, and delivery of merchandise and materials to the production site directly with the Brand.
- Any delays in this coordinating process will have an impact on the deliverables already agreed upon and the Brand must be updated ahead of time by the agency team member.

d. Story Development

- Script writing or episodic outline will take place during the preproduction phase.
- Scripts or outlines will be delivered for Brand and Agency review in phases or stages.
- If feedback is needed from the client, a meeting can be scheduled to review the general script(s). The Branded Entertainment team is to participate.

- Scripts are to be approved by the Brand following a specific deadline.
- If more time is needed by the client, the Prod Co is to be notified in advance.

e. Name/Title for Content (Working Title)

Prod Co or Branded Entertainment team is to propose a list of options. The process is as follows:

Approval Process

- Prod Co works in conjunction with Agency and client and also takes into consideration suggestions from the Network/outlet.
- Network/media outlet may play a key role in determining final title of the content.
- Previous negotiations may have already taken place between Agency and Network. If that is the case, Prod Co is to be notified as soon as possible.

Deadline for Approval of Show Title

- Decision to have a final title must be reached *before* moving into production.
- Rights and clearances have been approved by legal.

Credits

At this stage, but most definitely *prior to* going into post-production, duly note if a client agrees and can make the decision about receiving production credits. (*Note*: At times the client may agree to the production credits, but the decision is to come from above. Production credits are to be something the client wants, but also something they can decide in favor of.)

STAGE III: PRODUCTION, POSTPRODUCTION, AND ADDITIONAL REQUESTS

- Estimate the timing required to complete production (principal photography).
- Postproduction assumptions to follow include:
  - Estimate a schedule to finalize rough cuts and a period required for notes. Include the amount of time suggested to return notes to postproduction.
  - Once rough cuts are finalized, address the number of rounds of notes required from the Agency, Brand, and Network.
  - Maintain a record of who has reviewed the content and the turnaround time.
  - Maintain a record of any additional materials or branded product required to produce while in postproduction, e.g., sales tapes, materials, presentation reels, etc. must be either allocated as a line item on the approved budget or invoiced separately.

- If additional requests are made by the client, and these requests impact delivery deadlines, the Agency must address the issue directly with the Brand and the Network and revise deadlines with Prod Co.
- Overages and underages in the approved budget are to be addressed in the agreement, including how they will be handled between the two parties initiating a potential deal. An estimate of overages needs to be submitted prior to final delivery.

Note: These guidelines must be filled in on a term sheet with the proper dates, deliverables, and numbers corresponding to a specific deal.

APPENDIX 1

TERMINOLOGY

Due to the nature of a business that is still in the process of evolving, including a list of terms that defines the business itself is necessary to maintain absolute clarity about Branded Entertainment deals and transactions. Certain terms are loosely used in the industry. Some may understand these terms very well, but others, such as newcomers to the media industry, may need to have an understanding of the meaning of certain basic terms.

Brand: Refers to the leading member(s) from a company who actively participate(s) in the process of the pitch, the proposal, and the budget as one of the contracting parties (Chapter 3 has a complete description of who the brand is. Later chapters reference the brand as one of the participating parties.)

Branded Content Idea (BCI): An idea that morphs into content that can be produced for an audience with a consumer brand intertwined into its core message. Brand inclusion is at the starting point of this content.

Branded Deal (BD): The final agreement reached by the contracting parties in regard to the content produced for the media with brand inclusion.

Branded Idea (BI): An idea that has a consumer brand attached to it. Commercials start as a branded idea. The brand is also at the start of the process. A branded idea also means that the idea and the brand are together from the start. If the branded idea can be developed into content, it can become a branded content idea.

Branded Team (BT): The group of people assigned to participate in the creation and execution of a branded deal. The branded team is usually comprised of members from the different contracting parties.

Client: Refers to a consumer brand company or a conglomerate of multiple brands such as a package goods company (Colgate-Palmolive) or a service-driven entity (an insurance company). These companies are the ultimate client(s) in a branded deal. They are also the clients of an agency, a media outlet, and a production company. (In the traditional media world, an agency is also a client to a media outlet or a media outlet can also be the client of a production company.)

Content Idea (CI): An idea that has the possibility of being turned into content for the media. A content idea is what an audience consumes when they go to a media outlet to be informed or entertained. A content idea can be short-form, mid-form, or long-form. A content idea can be designed in a sequence of chapters, called episodes, which turns into a series. A content idea can also be created as a one-time-only episode (O-T-O) or as a nugget for the web (webisodes, a vignette).

A Creative: A member of the branded team tasked with the goal of fleshing out ideas and deliberating among a group of these ideas until one idea appears to fulfill the brand objectives while also remaining entertaining to viewers, thus being able to also fulfill the client's objectives (a brand; a brand representative such as an agency or a network).

A Decoder: A decoder is a member of the branded team who, once an idea comes to life, will create a process for the brand to find all the touch points where the brand connects with each viewer. The decoder understands the ratio between creativity and the financial parameters outlined in the potential branded deal.

Gatekeeper: Common term used to refer to key employees who can give or deny access to key decision makers within an organization.

Idea: A concept that may have acceptance with a certain consumer. An idea can become a seed that will give birth to media content. An idea can be a seed for a commercial. An idea can also be the seed for branded media content.

An Implementer: A member of the branded team who is responsible for the viability and support of the branded idea by creating marketing "noise" and awareness in the world of consumers. A media background from multiple media outlets (TV, digital, print, etc.) is ideal for this role.

Notes: Comments, revisions, and suggestions made to the content document by key decision-making executives. Once an idea moves to content creation, it develops into a document that tells the story in detail. This document is revised by executives who are key decision makers. (Rough cuts from the newly created content go through a similar review in the process of editing. Notes at this time are from those with final green-light authority. Their comments are then used for revisions that eventually generate a final cut.)

Pitch: In the Branded Entertainment business, pitch is the official process by which an idea is presented to another party. The pitch illustrates how an idea can turn into content. The pitch can contain colorful examples that vivify what the content will look like once it comes to life. A pitch can also be the process by which the proposed content and a media outlet are intertwined together to fully engage one of the two. For instance, the idea may have already been sold to the brand but not to the network. By pitching the idea with the proposed content and the network already together, the network may be fully on board.

Product Placement: The business of brand inclusion within entertainment. This is the practice that preceded Branded Entertainment. The focus of product placement is to make visible a brand logo or a brand name. No major creative work is done to put a brand inside content.

Short-, Mid-, and Long-Form Content: The final length of the content produced measured in minutes or seconds designed for any network or media outlet: short (3 to 5 minutes or less); mid (11 minutes); and long (22 or 44 minutes). These standardized numbers of minutes take the format terminology of a commercialized hour of media content on air or online, known to consumers as a half-hour or a 1-hour show or a 1-hour episode.

Touch Points: A marketing term frequently used to refer to the places where consumers come into contact with a brand message—where the marketing of the brand connects with the consumer (billboard ads, consumer events such as a concert, a VIP experience with a celebrity, door-to-door advertising, a featured radio promotion, etc.).

Treatment: The document that outlines the arc of a story designed for TV, movies, or books; a short summary that contains pivotal points of the story. A treatment can also be an outline for a series presenting the story arc plus the key elements of each episode in a potential series. A treatment can be done for scripted or unscripted content.

In the chapters that explain the assembly of a deal, contractual terminology is used with a legal process that needs to be engaged once a deal is ready to be inked.

Contracting Parties: Entities (parties) that participate in the creation, production, and/or dissemination of a particular content with brand inclusion:

- Media outlets/networks/consumer platforms
- Consumer brand companies or conglomerates known as consumer goods
- Advertising agencies, creative shops, and time buying services
- Production companies

Flow: The sequential process to be carried out when a deal travels from party to party to be reviewed and approved.

Funding or Cash Infusion: The money required to create a branded deal. The funding or cash infusion can come from one or more than one contracting party.

Media Outlet Deal: An agreement reached by a media outlet or network in regards to a particular content to be licensed or owned with the purpose of being watched and consumed by the media audience. A media outlet deal does not have to have brand inclusion.

Metrics: Systems designed to measure performance, management of cash, and success. Metrics in the Branded Entertainment business need to be customized according to the goals of the contracting parties.

Transaction Deal (Agreements): A portion of a legal deal reached between two of the parties that form part of a branded deal. Several transaction deals or agreements may need to be concluded before reaching a branded deal.

Working Budget: A prearranged sum of money destined for a particular goal of one of the parties. A network may have a working budget for content in a particular time period. A brand may have a working budget for any efforts on television. A production company may have a working budget preset for an idea to be executed into content.

APPENDIX 2

Branded Entertainment Sample Term Sheet Template

Once negotiations reach a pivotal moment moving toward a deal, a term sheet can be a starting point to memorialize key business points. This term sheet can be binding or non-binding. If binding, obtaining signatures from the parties listed at the end of the term sheet are a must. If non-binding, one party can sign off on the agreement and then send the term sheet to the other parties for approval.

Main terms may include key business points that require more elaborate language to simplify the requirements and liabilities. Time tables may also be included as attachments to this initial term sheet.

In the example term sheet, a production entity and an advertising agency have agreed to ink the first term sheet that will then be reviewed by the brand's management team. If this term sheet awards an approval, the next move will be to move toward contractual terms.

DEAL POINTS FOR THE AGREEMENT:

1. AGENCY will receive an agency exclusive on branded integration in "SERIES X" (Working Title: X) during its first season and first right of refusal for its second season [fifteen (15) days to renew from the date the second season is picked up by the Network].

2. A maximum of three (3) categories from client roster will be integrated into the show. [EXAMPLES: automotive; telecommunications; and a third to be determined]

   a. *Note*: Final product categories must be cleared by the Network prior to finalizing agreement.

   b. Clients will receive full category exclusivity on Branded Entertainment integrations.

3. Each AGENCY client (BRAND) will receive:

   a. One (1) Storyline Integration [to be approved by BRAND]

   b. One (1) Logo Integration throughout the Show [Brand Presence]
      - Stadium Signage
      - Brand Usage Integration

   c. Digital Rights Extensions

   d. Point of Sale (POS) Rights [Visuals on brand POS strategies]

   e. Rights to an On-Line Sweepstakes [one (1) for all three (3) clients]

   f. Access to Talent [Talent fees and cost of travel are NOT included.]
      - Should client request special talent to be included in the series, talent fees and travel-related costs must be covered by client (BRAND).

g. Inclusion in All Public Relations (PR) Materials

h. Logo Signage at Live Events through Step and Repeat

4. The Network under consideration and all evaluations are based on Network X, Weekday Primetime:

a. Airdate is scheduled to start in MONTH X, YEAR X.

5. Total Commitment Required: <u>$X net</u>

a. Payment Terms are in three (3) installments:

- 50% upon signing contract
- 25% in MONTH X, YEAR X
- 25% in MONTH X, YEAR X

b. Total value of media components alone is $X [APPROXIMATE VALUATION].

STORYLINE INTEGRATION:

Each client (BRAND) will receive a maximum X minutes per episode in which the BRAND is organically integrated into one (1) or more of the characters' lives. This package is for a total of X episodes for the aforementioned SERIES (Working Title: X):

- The AGENCY'S responsibility is to provide relevant copy points and transport of product to production locations at the client's expense.
- Give notes/details on the approximate production locations. [Include a timetable if available.]

LOGO INTEGRATION:

Beyond the storyline integration, BRAND may appear through a variety of elements throughout the show such as:
- Stadium Signage
- Outdoor Signage (street and in retail locations)
- Product Placement

Note: Creative materials/copy points must be approved by client (BRAND) and provided by AGENCY.

MEDIA EVALUATION ON INTEGRATIONS:

Estimated value for XX minutes of integration for a total of X episodes for an average of XX minutes per episode:
- XX minutes = XXX seconds equivalent to XX : 30s [30 seconds]
- TOTAL RATING POINTS (TRPs): XX × XX average RATING on Men 18–49 = XXX TRPs
- XX (:30s) × $XXX average Weekday Prime Rate = $XXXX value/BRAND
- Notes:
  - This valuation is based on estimated values and estimated time periods (from targeted Network).
  - These numbers are meant to demonstrate top value of branded integrations within a show.
  - These rates are non-negotiated commercial rates; they do not represent a guaranteed TRP delivery for the show. (*Note*: This valuation helps Media Managers process numbers most efficiently especially if the budget being used is an allocation from the media budget.)

DIGITAL PACKAGE:

Brand inclusion will be on the show's official website, which will reside as a standalone on the web or as a SERIES X Channel on XX Digital Address [for a period of XX months].

1. Promotional Elements:
   - Co-Branded media bank weight on XX digital space (SERIES X + BRAND) to drive males or females (adjust according to the BRAND's target.) directly to the show channel; hyper-targeting capabilities

2. Branding Elements:
   - Show X Channel Look and Feel: Background design can organically integrate BRAND's images from a real episode.
   - In-Channel Banners: Drives traffic to BRAND'S website.
   - Pre Rolls: BRAND spots play automatically when landing on the show's channel.

3. Contests:
   - Encourage users to vote on videos that have been submitted to a contest.

4. In-Video Commentary:
   - Add BRAND interactive commentary to SERIES X videos.

5. Invitations:
   - Users invite other digital channel X users to watch SERIES X videos while they are watching them.

6. Branded Chats:
   - A tool that allows users to chat with others who are watching the same SERIES X video they are watching.

7. Syndication:
   - Show channel can live on any website in addition to digital channel X.
8. Functionality:
   - When a user arrives at SERIES X Show X Channel, the featured video plays automatically.
9. Digital Package Value:
   - XX per client for a total value of $XX [Similar valuation principles to TV apply.]
   - *Note*: AGENCY is responsible for providing artwork and BRAND/Logo usage guidelines.

OTHER ELEMENTS INCLUDED IN THE AGREEMENT:

- Point of Sale (POS) Rights:
  - Pass-Through Rights to utilize official images from the show at the POS on- and off-premise
- Public Relations:
  - Inclusion of BRAND mentioned in all show-related PR materials/Logo signage at live events through Step and Repeat

Note: This sample term sheet must be filled out with the proper dates, deliverables, and numbers corresponding to a specific deal.

By: Company Name

By: _____

Name:

Title:

INDEX